STUDIES IN MODERN EUROPEAN LITERATURE
AND THOUGHT

General Editor:

ERICH HELLER

*Professor of German
in the University College of Swansea*

GUSTAVE FLAUBERT

Other titles are in preparation

GUSTAVE FLAUBERT

AND THE ART OF REALISM

BY

ANTHONY THORLBY

NEW HAVEN
YALE UNIVERSITY PRESS
1957

CONTENTS

J'obéis à une fatalité supérieure.

I lead a bitter life devoid of all external joy, with nothing to keep me going but a kind of perpetual fury, which cries sometimes from helplessness, but which never ceases. I love my work with the frenzied and perverse love of an ascetic for his hair shirt . . . I hate myself and blame myself for this madness of pride that makes me pant after a chimera . . . (But) sometimes I have glimpsed a state of soul far superior to life, beside which glory and even happiness count for nothing . . . (Then) sometimes I feel profound ennui, a great emptiness, doubts that laugh in my face, even while I am enjoying the simplest satisfaction. Well, what of it! I would not exchange all this for anything, because in my conscience it seems that I am doing my duty, that I obey a higher fatality, that I do what is good and that I am in the right.

(C, II, 394 f.)[1]

Every book written on Flaubert has commented on the fact that he was both a realist and a romantic. Does this mean simply that he was unusually versatile? Indeed, the measure of his greatness may partly be his sensitiveness to both realms of experience; but to neglect his awareness of their fundamental conflict is to underestimate his accomplishment. For he resolved it ultimately, not by alternating between a romantic and a realistic vein of writing, but by creating a new style out of the very heart of discord. Flaubert's letter describing his labours on *Madame Bovary* shows him practising the art of realism in a truly romantic turmoil of soul.

The word 'realism', however, may in itself be misleading. Most literature is realistic – depending, of course, on what is experienced as real. The perennial facts of life are probably always much the same, only literature reflects ever new ways of experiencing them. Description of external appearances alone is scarcely a distinguishing feature of any particular style; what matters is the importance, or meaning, attributed to them. The choice of subject matter, perhaps, might distinguish the realism of much modern fiction, which tells home truths in common or garden surroundings. In this way it undoubtedly strikes home, particularly to the contemporary reader; but it is not automatically a truer way of recognizing life 'for what

1 The reference is to *La Correspondance de Gustave Flaubert* (9 vols), Paris, Louis Conard, 1926-1933 (abbreviated as C).

it is'. All artificialities of poetic form may have been done away with, and yet even in the simplest reportage the basically creative, symbolic features of the written word prove to be ineradicable. Statements without any form at all would be literally nonsense; and it will be found, in fact, that a realist, using such a discursive, explicit form as the novel, has to make a far more deliberate act of interpretation than do poets in a formal style (where a lot of the thinking is, so to speak, done for them by the conventions of their genre). A strict empiricism would not know where to begin or end on a virtually infinite range of possible scrutiny, even supposing it could find an entirely impartial way of writing down its findings. By the time a complete and coherent shape has been given to a novel, the selection, placing, focus of quite ordinary, factual details reflect the artist's vision of the nature of reality. His realism will have become a creative definition of what things really matter in his experience.

Flaubert was extremely sensitive to the implications of artistic coherence, of style and form. A study of his work must surely make clear the degree to which realism implies a 'definition' of reality. His achievement as a realist emerges as the result of a complex labour, involving both the form and the content of his novels, and reflecting his intuition of a radical change in the structure of traditional values, not only aesthetic, but also philosophical and moral. Born in 1821, he grew up to discover that the romantic phase of that change was over. The romantic reaction against the conventional realities of classical literature had made intensity of personal feeling the criterion of 'real' significance, the yearning for some undefined inner experience, adventurous, remote, exotic, mystical—everything, in fact, except one thing, which Flaubert considered to be reality itself. The definition is negative, but this was essentially how Flaubert himself characterized the real: as a world in which human feelings and ideas are *not* of any real significance. He wrote, for instance:

I do not know, and nobody knows, what those two words mean: body and soul, where one finishes and the other begins. We are aware of *forces* and that is all. Materialism and spiritualism weigh too heavily still on the science of man for all these phenomena to be studied impartially. The anatomy of the human heart has not yet been worked out. How do you expect to be cured? The unique glory of the nineteenth century will be to have undertaken this study. The *historical*

sense is still a new thing in the world. Now ideas will be studied as facts, and beliefs will be dissected like organisms.
(C, IV, 314)

Science and history: these, Flaubert declared, were the 'two muses of modern times'. The research he undertook before writing *Salammbô* or *Bouvard et Pécuchet* would have done credit to a historian, while he worked to give his style the precision of a scientific analysis. Inevitably he has been criticized for an untrue, even immoral, use of facts; but the objection misses the point. Flaubert was not interested in any of the conclusions of science or history; he was interested in their method, which seemed to him to exclude the possibility of maintaining any relevant beliefs about the value of human existence. They discovered, he believed, a pure idea of the real, free from all illusions about the metaphysical reality of the spirit. He envisaged the goal of art as identical with that of science, and prescribed for the writer the absolute impartiality of the scientist:

What is so fine about the natural sciences is that they do not wish to prove anything. What a wealth of facts they enjoy, and what an immense field of thought! Human beings must be treated like mastodons and crocodiles; why get excited about the horn of the former or the jaw of the latter? Display them, stuff them, bottle them, that's all–but appraise or evaluate them: no! And who are you anyway, *petits crapauds*?
(C, III, 154)

Thus Flaubert's comment that *Madame Bovary* was a work of 'criticism' should not be understood in a moral, or even a sociological, sense; he was always careful to avoid any didactic tendency. The criticism which his style exhibited was more in the nature of an epistemological critique. Flaubert had no theory to offer, either psychological or sociological. Had he had one, his style might have been a great deal more conventional, as is Zola's. Zola wrote fiction in order (partly) to prove his point. For Flaubert the process of writing fiction was itself the point. It was the method, not the conclusion, that mattered. Zola assumed some of the conclusions of science to be true and set about exploiting their aesthetic possibilities. Flaubert realized the spiritual implications and requirements of the scientific method, and made his writing an exercise in the discovery of truth. It is for this reason that a unique place may be claimed for him in the history of literature.

9

Flaubert's idealisation of science may sound a little naive when taken at face value. But there is always something of a grimace about it, and many of his observations have the ring of paradoxical *boutades*. His expectation of truth in the nineteenth century must be read in connection with comments of this kind: 'The eighteenth century denied the *soul*, and the achievement of the nineteenth will perhaps be to have killed *man* himself'. Flaubert knew that a serious problem confronted not only the spirit of man but also the future of art, in the aesthetic he was proposing. At the time when he first conceived the plans that were to materialise in *Madame Bovary* and *Salammbô*, he wrote:

> Alas! it seems to me that when one dissects so well children still to be born, one is no longer in a fit state to create them. My metaphysical acuity alarms me terribly.   (C, II, 254)

The list of such doubts is endless, but one further example may be quoted to point to yet another difficulty, this time with regard to *L'Education sentimentale:*

> What profoundly distresses me is the conviction I have o doing something useless, I mean contrary to the very aim of art, which is to achieve a vague exaltation. For with the scientific demands that are made nowadays and a bourgeois subject, the book seems to me to be radically impossible. Beauty is not compatible with modern life, and this is the last time I will have anything to do with it: I have had enough.
>
> The monks' hope is in vain: the sun is not on their side. For nothing is eternal, not even the sun itself. And we, wretched little grains of dust, paltry vibrations of an immense movement, lost atoms!—let us join together our two nothingnesses in a common tremor, and let it be as endless as space. What a metaphysic!   (C, V, 260)

It is against this background that the well-known portrait of Flaubert the artist appears: the hermit of Croisset, leading a life of ascetic denial out of dedication to an art that tortured him. He suffered from a 'hatred of life', and considered the artist 'a monstrosity, something outside nature'. When his mother asked him if he had any intention of marrying, he scorned the idea of himself 'fulfilling the conditions of humanity'. Poets, like priests, do not marry; and to participate in the world is to become the 'dupe' of the works of God.

You can depict wine, love, women, glory, on condition that you do not become a drunkard, a lover, a husband, a soldier. You see life badly when you are actually in it, you suffer from it, or enjoy it too much. (C, II, 268)

The real significance of statements of this kind is likely to escape us if we believe that they simply extol the virtues of the contemplative life. These virtues are traditionally vindicated by a faith in something that is more valuable than the life of action. Yet Flaubert was never consistent in claiming any higher value for the object of his devotion. He saw himself as 'a mystic who believes in nothing'. His meditations on the question of how any significant truth or beauty may attach to even the most inspired idea of a valueless world are inconclusive; and his feelings show the strain of a lasting doubt whether his devotion to so paradoxical an ideal of truth might not be a frenzy of diabolical destructiveness. Above all, the exercise of the artistic imagination, for which his precepts sound sometimes so deceptively simple, was being burdened with a new and almost unheard-of responsibility. It had, so to speak, to create *ex nihilo*, to create something of significance which would yet be true to a genuine conviction of nothingness.

The lesser consequences of this paradox can be seen even in Flaubert's simple assertion that:

The less one feels a thing, the better qualified one is to express it as it is (as it is always, in itself, as a universal apart from its ephemeral contingencies). But one must have the faculty for making oneself feel it. (C, II, 462)

The function of the imagination is to be, in a peculiarly absolute sense, *purely* artistic. It is remarkable to what lengths of research and observation Flaubert went to gather the smallest detail of his material. In fact, he seems at times to have deliberately sought material for which his imagination could have no real sympathy or spontaneous feeling: as though to make quite sure that the only passion entering his work would be for style alone. In practise, of course, the fact that style must also be expressing the appearance of something could not be glossed over. This did not prevent Flaubert, however, from wishing that it could, wishing to write 'a book about nothing, a book without any external connection, which would support itself by internal force of style'. (C, II, 345)

Flaubert is not being entirely whimsical. Though he could

11

not write a book about nothing, his style reflects his sense of the nothingness of life. Many analyses have been made of his grammatical and syntactical usages, to show his mastery of French prose and rank him with the finest stylists. Flaubert himself claimed allegiance to the classical preceptors of the French language and wished that the problems of style might again be regulated according to some such clear, aesthetic principles as had once been laid down by Boileau and Buffon. But to praise Flaubert purely for his formal virtuosity is perhaps to ignore his realization of the fate of poetry and literature in an age of 'realism'. For though he wished that he could create 'pure phraseology' and believe 'as a Platonist' that the 'law of numbers governs the sentiments and images of poetry', he knew the answer even as he wrote:

> If I pursue this train of thought very far, I end up by not being able to see anything at all; for, looked at from the other side, art has got to be human.   (C, VII, 294)

The human, however, presented itself as a sickening experience of what Flaubert called 'la bêtise humaine'. Blaming himself for his 'madness of pride', he yet aspired to a vision of beauty and truth that would reward him with 'a state of soul far superior to life'. From the very start of his career as a writer he was puzzled by the ambiguous source of his inspiration, which expressed itself both as a passion for beauty and as a sense of spiritual destitution in the world and even, to some extent, in his own life. At the time when he began La Tentation de St. Antoine, his first serious work, he wrote to his friend Maxime Du Camp:

> I am going to get down to work at last! at last! I want, and I hope, to be hard at it for a long time and without respite. Is this because I have felt directly the vanity of ourselves, of our plans, of our happiness, of beauty, of goodness, of everything? But I have the impression of being a very limited and mediocre person ... I believe I can produce good things, but I always ask myself the question, what is the good? Which is all the more curious because I do not feel myself discouraged. On the contrary, I turn more than ever towards the pure idea, towards the infinite. I aspire to it, it attracts me, I become a Brahmin, or rather I become a little mad.
> (C, I, 203)

Flaubert obviously had no desire to elaborate a philosophy in his letters to his friends; but his correspondence reveals, in fact, his awareness of a genuine metaphysical problem. What was the nature of being when it could inspire both unlimited aspiration and total despair? What was the nature of the spirit which, Flaubert claimed, could rest, like God, 'suspended in the infinite', when the infinite was something which 'submerges all our conceptions, and from the moment that *it* is, why should there be any purpose or point in anything so relative as us?' Or in more personal terms, what was the connection between the ascetic zeal with which he pursued chimeric nuances of style and that 'holocaust of infernal disgust' that plagued him the while, as the demons plagued St. Antony, until sublimity was confused with 'the drunkenness of a perpetual orgy'? Flaubert's discursive answers are as fragmentary as the questions; his true answer lay in his rare masterpieces (and also his failures), where the ambiguities are finally rendered with the clarity of an idea. Yet even from some of his discursive passages we may notice that his sense of writing from a direct feeling of the vanity of everything matured into a view of genius as a refinement of suffering.

> In proportion as man rises in the scale of creatures, so his nervous faculty increases, that is to say, the faculty for suffering. Suffering and thought would then be the same thing? Genius is perhaps no more than a refinement of suffering, that is, a more complete and intense penetration of the objective world through our soul. The sadness of Molière came from all the human folly which he felt within himself... The mountains for Michelangelo had a soul, their nature corresponded to his, it was like the sympathy of two analogous elements; but this would establish, I don't know where or how, some sort of volcanic trails (subterranean connections) of an inconceivable magnitude, which would shatter the poor human frame. (C, III, 358 f.)

A passage like this expresses the complementary thought to Flaubert's more exalted notion of the artist, whose genius, 'suspended in the infinite', aspires to the pure idea. If it is possible to consider these, and Flaubert's other, scattered, comments as a whole, they will be found to exhibit traces of a feature common to most romantic aesthetics: the artist in some sort of cosmic role of mediation. The concept depends upon a rediscovery, such as Flaubert had made, of a striking

13

antithesis between truth and existence. Out of the endless process of existence and the otherwise vain human striving for individuality and self-importance, there is also produced a faculty for spiritual suffering, what Flaubert calls the penetration of the objective world into the soul. Thus the artist, who has achieved the greatest refinement of suffering, has an inner kinship with the whole scale of creation from mountains to man, and in his soul the image of existence crystallizes into an idea. This is the source of Flaubert's idealism. He was inspired by the hope of some kind of uniquely aesthetic virtue attaching to the realization of the world *as* an idea.

The metaphysical implications of this situation belong to the history of philosophy, where they may be best understood perhaps in the work of Schopenhauer (some of whose writings Flaubert is known to have read). In itself the situation explains many aspects of Flaubert's thought, and points to the intellectual dilemma behind his personal sense of suffering and his constant assertion that art and life are incompatible. How in practise an artist is ever to mediate between these extremes, which are characterized in such uncompromisingly opposite terms, and from his experience of the vanity of everything actually create forms both beautiful and true is a question that might well prompt fears for the capacity of 'the poor human frame'.[1]

Thus behind the usual sociological explanation of Flaubert's dislike for contemporary society there lies a profounder reason why, in his near total absorption in his art, he felt himself isolated from life.

> There is now such a huge gap between myself and the rest of the world that I am amazed sometimes to hear the most natural and simple things spoken. The most banal word holds me in singular admiration. There are gestures and tones of voice from which I cannot distract my attention, and stupidities which give me a sense of nausea.   (C, I, 192)

It sounds as if Flaubert, standing on the farthest boundary of the real in his yearning for transcendence, had lost his sense of spiritual perspective. And while his obsession with the nuances

---

[1] With regard to his sense of his own individuality, Flaubert expressed two interestingly different ideas. On the one hand he was fascinated by what he called the 'necromancy of self', felt annihilated by the thought of time as 'an immense precipice hanging over the vortex of nothingness, forever dividing you from yourself'. On the other hand, as part of the ever-living universe he can believe that in his imagination he has 'existed' for ever. I have memories that go back to the Pharaohs ... The individual I am now is the result of the individualities I have lost'.

of style has sometimes been taken and hailed as genuine spiritual devotion, his obsession with trivialities, and even clichés, of thought and feeling has also inspired criticism and regret. But is there not, after all, a connection? In a situation where truth and existence were mutually exclusive, and significance separate from reality, the impact of the most simple and natural things could be enormous, simply by being real. They became, so to speak, symbols of untruth. As symbols they fulfilled one of the essential conditions of art: an identity of meaning and material. Only, the meaning was negative and, from the critical point of view from which Flaubert viewed the aesthetic significance of a cliché, abstract. And while his mind contemplated a pure expression of negative truth, his feelings were overwhelmed with nausea and disgust.

Flaubert was under no illusion about the limitations of such an ambiguously 'pure art'. He regretted that it was no longer possible to believe in 'the reality of poetry in life, in the plastic beauty of the passions, etc.', and he foresaw that the future would place art 'somewhere in the middle between algebra and music'. He was impressed by the 'instinct for life' in the great classics of renaissance literature, praised the vitality of *Gargantua et Pantagruel* and said of such authors as Cervantes and Shakespeare that 'they do not need to practise the art of style . . . it is we who count only by virtue of accomplished execution'. What he admired in *Don Quixote* was 'the absence of art and the perpetual fusion of reality and illusion', a definition which throws his own concept of art into the sharpest relief.

Flaubert's admiration for *Don Quixote* has led to suggestions of influence and similarity with regard to *Madame Bovary*. The weakness of this approach is to rely too much on superficial resemblances and to neglect the obvious, though less easily definable, difference between works so unlike in tone and stature. Undoubtedly, each novel is based on a contrast between illusion and reality, and each marks a fresh discovery in what realism can accomplish in fiction; but neither the contrast nor the realism is the same in both cases. Flaubert's peculiar style of realism will be discussed later, but the point may be made here in general terms.

Indeed, both Don Quixote and Emma Bovary are a prey to delusion; and it might be said that the point of the realism in both books is to show up this delusion for what it is. The result, however, is quite different in each case. Cervantes leaves us smiling at his hero's incongruous application of genuine ideals, whereas Flaubert leaves us in uncertainty and doubt about the worth of his heroine's sentimental idealizations. For all the debunking, Don Quixote's illusions do preserve a kind of significance, full of real echantment, humour, pathos and love, which Emma's illusions lack; his remain, so to speak, truly 'quixotic', while hers are disastrously wedded to that kind of 'Bovary-ism' which, in French, became almost a by-word for the tawdry and the stupid. The two are not, in fact, deluded in anything like the same way.

The difference, surely, lies in this: Don Quixote is misled by his imagination, Emma by her feelings. In the case of Cervantes the contrast is between the real and the ideal, in the case of Flaubert it is between reality and sentiment. And whereas the world is enhanced with each new stroke of Don Quixote's indomitable imaginative ingenuity, it grows more silly and sordid with each more desperate flutter of Emma's emotions. For the still lovable humanity of the still lovable knight is brought out only the more clearly by contrast with his delusions of grandeur (what figure of chivalry was ever so endearing?); and this in spite of the fact that his particular version of the ideal cannot be taken literally. On the other hand, the scales are weighted increasingly against Emma Bovary by the exhaustion of her emotional vitality; the exposure of her sentimental delusions as they actually are begins to cast doubt on the worth of feelings as such, by suggesting that the belief which they inspire, whether in happiness or in any kind of spiritual value, is literally unreal. Hence it is that, while Cervantes' realism bestows immortal life upon Don Quixote's illusions, Flaubert's realism damns forever Madame Bovary's life of feeling.

Flaubert's paradoxical comment on the 'absence of art' in *Don Quixote* points to the different ways in which each writer has presented the contrast between illusion and reality. Cervantes treated it as a real contrast, plain for everyone (except the hero) to see, as one of the great humorous truths of life. For Flaubert feelings and ideas were on a level with everything else, and to lend them any real distinction was impossible; so that (in theory, at least) their apparent contrast had to be interpreted 'purely aesthetically', as an ironical truth of style, the perception of which depended on the subtlest nuance of word and phrase. In the same way, impersonality for Cervantes was simply a cultured gesture of self-effacement behind his material, whereas for Flaubert it was a perpetual struggle for a special kind of stylistic detachment. And whereas Cervantes' reassuring point of view is really apparent and only pretends to be disguised, Flaubert's point of view is deliberately ambiguous and only appears to be sustaining the sympathies necessary to his story. For in order to write fiction at all, Flaubert felt bound to preserve the conventional forms of interest; but how he complained of his weariness with the, to him, mere formalities of plot, suspense, dénouement and so forth! And in his last work, *Bouvard et Pécuchet*, the illusion of an interesting fiction is barely maintained.

One further aspect of Flaubert's 'philosophy' remains to be considered. He acknowledged religion and art as 'the two great manifestations of the Idea', but realized that, in the absence of anything to believe in, or any 'real' beauty in the world, they depended upon a kind of pure assertion of the spirit, which he characterized in both the artist and the saint as fanaticism. He introduced this notion in a letter where he had begun by praising Voltaire as a fanatic in the cause of truth, and contrasted the passion of that sceptic's ideal: 'Ecrasons l'infame', with the feeble profession of scepticism in the smallminded Voltaireans who merely belittled great things. Flaubert claimed Voltaire as a saint and professed himself his disciple, a true religious soul, though without a God.

> For fanaticism is religion; and the philosophers of the eighteenth century [Flaubert is excluding Voltaire from this category] in denouncing the one destroyed the other. Fanaticism is faith, faith in itself, the burning faith which acts and produces great works. (C, III, 148)

And in another letter:

> What draws me above all things is religion. I mean all religions, not one rather than another. Each dogma on its own repels me, but I consider the feeling that created them as the most natural and poetical in humanity. I don't like philosophers who find them only fraud and foolishness.
>
> (C, IV, 170)

That realism conflicted with the truths of religion was to Flaubert no ground for facile optimism, or for believing in the progress of social enlightenment. He understood too clearly the dilemma of finding a real basis for evaluating the desires of the spirit, when the old values appeared unreal. Thus he could write to George Sand: 'I execrate what is generally called realism, even though I am supposed to be one of its pontifs: figure that

17

one out!' The answer is found, perhaps, in a passage like the following:

> I find that man is now more of a fanatic than ever, but fanatical for himself. He knows no other song, and his thought which has leapt beyond the suns, devoured the sky and (as Montaigne would have said) has bleated for the infinite, now finds no greater object than the wretchedness of real life, which it has tried continually to transcend. Thus France, since 1830, has been the raving victim of a senseless realism. The infallibility of universal suffrage is about to become dogma, which will succeed that of papal infallibility. Brute force, the law of number, the favour of the crowd, have succeeded the authority of name, divine law and the supremacy of the spirit. (C, III, 414)

The crucial phrase is 'a senseless realism'; a realism, that is to say, with no spiritual integrity, which merely serves the interests of human weakness. Flaubert believed in the possibility of a kind of 'pure' fanaticism, with the strength to match itself against the senselessness of life and to survive. In this respect he anticipated the various existentialist endeavours to reassert the supremacy of the spirit, which have become familiar in the twentieth century, and which Nietzsche formulated in their most impressive form a decade after Flaubert. It is interesting that the Franco-Prussian war, which precipitated Nietzsche's disgust for the Germans, also confirmed Flaubert's despair of the French. The three great evolutions of history, he wrote, have been 'Paganism, Christianity and Brutism (Muflisme) . . . We are now witnessing the extinction of Latin culture'. Both Flaubert and Nietzsche, faced with this painful prospect of disintegration, tried fanatically to find in the very experience itself the enduring strength of an independent integrity. Flaubert's aesthetic mysticism, founded on a belief in nothing (unless disgust at the nothingness of man), teaches the soul a concentration of spiritual enthusiasm which will not be dependent on any of the idols of the world. Like Nietzsche's superhuman hero, man will rise superior to the recurrent illusions of history by accepting a universe beyond good and evil. It is the contemplation of this universe that Flaubert set as the ideal object of art:

> Let us bewail nothing; to complain of everything which afflicts or irritates us is to complain of the very nature of

18

existence. We who are artists are here to depict it and nothing more. Let us be religious in spirit . . . the sun always shines for the strong in heart who place themselves beyond the mountain tops. I am turning towards a kind of aesthetic mysticism. (C, III, 16)

He might almost be anticipating Nietzsche's *Also Sprach Zarathustra* as he continues:

> The time is near for the reappearance of universal languor, belief in the end of the world, in the coming of a Messiah. But in the present absence of theological support, where will the basis be found for this unconscious enthusiasm? Some will find it in the flesh, others in the old religions, others again in art; and humanity, like the lost tribe in the desert, will go and adore all manner of idols. (Ibid.)

Flaubert's obsession with the decadence of contemporary life, his almost perverse sense of stupidity, his fascination with the senseless and the cruel, were a kind of perpetual sacrifice of feeling, made in the name of a negatively conceived ideal, the unavoidably nihilistic terms in which he conceived the transcendent destiny of man.

> If the sense of human insufficiency, of the nothingness of life, were to perish (which would be the consequence of their [the socialists'] hypothesis), we would be more stupid than the birds, who at least perch on the trees. The soul is asleep at the moment, drunk with words it has heard before, but it will have a frenzied awakening when it will abandon itself to the joys of emancipation: for it will be embarrassed by no more limitations, neither of government or religion, nor by any formula whatever. Republicans of every shade strike me as the most primitive pedagogues in the world, dreaming of organisations, of legislation, of society as a nunnery. I believe, on the contrary, that in everything rules are disappearing, barriers being overthrown, and that the earth is levelling itself. This great confusion will perhaps bring freedom. (C, III, 17)

In the gloomy years that introduced the last decade of his life, Flaubert experienced, with morbid fascination, the death of many things, ideals and friends, hopes and memories. And he accepted its challenge with a motto that has the ring of Zara-

19

thustra's desperate message for survival: 'Par delà les tombes en avant!' Perhaps, he reflected, the most important thing that death has to teach us is life. In the very spectacle of spiritual annihilation Flaubert would learn a strength of spirit that can be measured against Nietzsche's ideal of superhuman fortitude:

Do not rebel against the idea of total oblivion. Invoke it rather! Those who are like us must have a religion of despair. One must be on a level with destiny, which is to be impassive like itself. By force of repeating to oneself 'It is so, it is so' and by contemplating the black emptiness one becomes calm. (C, IV, 341)[1]

These ideas however, scarcely appear in the content of his work, for although the creative process had to assert itself in the face of such 'nothingness', the ideas and feelings inspired by it could not be given spontaneous expression. Flaubert's ideal of impersonality was intended to rescue art from the pitfalls of a bewildered religious and philosophical sensitivity. But the simple resort to pure artistry ceased to be simple under the burden of a still heavy, but now inarticulate, sense of responsibility, while its purity became ambiguous. His art, created with such endless toil, at the expense of feeling and the natural grace of life, carried the stamp of a 'higher fatality'. It was the fatality neither of the romantic hero nor of the 'poète maudit', but of the modern mind which grimly determines to pursue an ideal of truth that is as indifferent to doubt as to belief, with nothing to sustain it except its own fury of determination. It was the fatality which made life seem the more futile, the more furiously Flaubert pursued his ideal, and which condemned his characters to this futility the more mercilessly as he sacrificed his own life to his art.

II

Flaubert's earliest works amount to a series of fragmentary confessions in imitation romantic style with such characteristic titles as *Agonies, Les Mémoires d'un fou,* and *Novembre: Fragments de style quelconque.* Like the less successful juvenilia of other writers, their interest is more documentary than literary; they

[1] cf. Correspondance, IV, 464

offer, apart from some biographical information, an interesting insight into the development of Flaubert's art. They are emotionally pretentious in their bid for intense imaginative experience, but at the same time self-conscious and genuinely doubtful about the value of all this inwardness. Flaubert realized that there was something of a pose in his cultivation of romantic feeling and played with the idea of whether he really meant it. How could he set himself up as a poet, when, 'speaking of the soul, he began to laugh'? That tormenting question as to the value of it all, which was to inspire his life-long search for an unquestionable form of artistic accomplishment, is the constant theme of his earliest writing. 'What is the good of learning the truth when it is bitter?' The question is merely elaborated in a variety of impassioned contrasts between all the exotic and erotic dreams of romantic adolescence and the bitter truth of misery and decay; but always with the doubt that an impassioned response is vain, because the 'human heart is lost in an enormous solitude', and the passions are but 'travellers in the desert'.

These sentiments are trite, but their weakness is revealing. It appears most strikingly in the theologically primitive conception of a scene (the first of several which lead up to *La Tentation de St. Antoine*) where Satan 'tempts' Christ with a vision of universal evil, debauch and hell. The issue is basically an aesthetic one. The romantic rediscovery of spiritual vitality in increasingly subjective terms began to find the objective reality of the spirit more and more remote and doubtful. In the extreme case experienced by Flaubert, his feelings were entirely negative. What inspired him was love which was not fulfilled, memories of lost childhood, a sense of infinitude which 'I wanted to embrace, but which annihilated me', the idea of poetry as no more than 'a comedy played before one's own heart', and the prospect of a world where the spirit is crushed by folly, corruption, cruelty and death—in fact, all the favourite themes of romantic literature. But if they were taken *really* seriously, Flaubert reflected, what *real* value is there in feeling anything about them at all? The question is considerably less primitive than Satan's temptation of Christ, which expresses it figuratively as a religious issue. For it reveals the emergence of a new concept of realism within the romantic mode of experience. The increased claims and seriousness of romantic poetry, which became, as Jacques Rivière put it, 'a raid on the infinite', and which made Flaubert love his work 'with the frenzied and perverse love of an ascetic for his hair shirt',

21

burdened the poetic imagination with new responsibilities proportionate to its expectations. The experience of poetry was supposed to have a peculiar significance; to be, in fact, the only true experience in life altogether, so that art and literature inevitably began to assume a metaphysical importance. Flaubert's question is asked at this pretentious level; he was measuring the significance of poetry *against* the ultimate realities of existence —only to find that his spiritual anticipation of 'poetry is everything' was in reality based on nothing.

Flaubert grew suspicious of the whole life of feeling and the conventional realms of romantic experience. For it seemed to him that such sentimental self-indulgence prevented him from earning any real experience of life. He has imagined love, beauty, glory, religion, but all these things have remained unrealized, and he is left with nothing except a wasted existence and the sense that he has been cheated of something, that he has exhausted the potentialities of life without ever *really* feeling anything.

> Devoured by limitless passions . . ., tempted by all the voluptuous pleasures of thought and desiring all the poetries, all the harmonies . . . I fell annihilated in an abyss of misery . . . I saw no longer anything, I felt nothing . . . I imagined that I had within me a supreme incarnation . . . and that these torments were the life of the god I bore in my entrails. To this magnificent god I sacrificed every hour of my youth; I made of myself a temple to contain a divinity, and the temple remained empty . . . I had no use for real life, and it used me up, consumed me. [1]

Flaubert's emotional overstraining to find even in this experience some real significance was self-defeating. The romantic yearning of the spirit was likely to end simply in a suicidal exhaustion of passion–the fate of Emma Bovary. Everywhere Flaubert perceived the compulsion of some feeling, 'freedom, belief, God, virtue', the illusions created by the soul to obscure the ultimate nothingness. When he wanted to leave the spectacle of his own miseries, all he could find was 'the same comedy perpetually repeated with the same actors'.

> The fatality which had oppressed me since my youth, now extended itself over the whole world; I watched it operate in all the actions of men as universally as the sun shines

[1] *Oeuvres de Jeunesse*, Conard, Paris, 1910; II, 180.

on the surface of the earth. It became for me a ghastly divinity which I adored as an Indian does the advancing Colossus that passes over his prostrate body. (Ibid. II, 184)

Flaubert's realism represents an attempt to express the illusions of feeling without making himself or his work the victim of illusion. It might not be possible to deal with the world in terms of feeling, but realistic fiction offered a way of treating feeling from the point of view of the world. In *La Tentation de St. Antoine* he is generally acknowledged to have made the greatest concession to romantic feeling, though its illusions are consistently portrayed as a kind of spiritual temptation. The work may be conveniently treated at the end of this section and his more clearly realistic ventures be looked at first. His conception of what the world and reality were was originally determined by the predicament of romantic feeling. Reality was misery, vice, illusion, folly–the predicament of feeling, in fact, looked at from the other side. Reality became interesting at just those points where the vain passions and thoughts of men were sacrificed to it.

There is already in Flaubert's *Novembre* a desire to analyse this reality dispassionately. The scene in which the hero is initiated into the sentimental facts of life as he lies in bed with a prostitute who tells him her story makes a crude mixture of romantic and realistic styles. There is at once the romantic sentiment for a woman who has lived for love, and a realistic sense of the frustration and hopelessness of the situation. The ideal of feeling which she symbolizes is matched against the cynical egoism of men and the commercial foolishness of women. The end of the book describes the hero in the third person, and this break in the narrative form from the first person marks an interesting development in Flaubert's literary career. For the immediate result is an almost complete loss of stature in the hero; when the lyrical passion and integrity of his feelings are taken away, he appears as an aimless young man futilely wasting away his life. Flaubert had found a way of ending his narrative, but not of resolving the problem of feeling.

The first *L'Education sentimentale* (1845) was, as the title suggests, to give fuller treatment to this problem, and it was also Flaubert's first full-length novel. The story is of a young man called Henry who comes to Paris full of extravagant expectations and engages in an adulterous love affair; he leaves behind him in his provincial home-town a friend called Jules, who reminds him of their youthful dreams. What Henry's

23

education teaches him is that reality does not correspond to expectation; what Jules' education teaches him is the unreality of the imaginative life. Again the narrative peters out, with the two friends meeting again in a state of aimless disillusion. Flaubert's new contribution to the problem lies in his understanding of the term 'sentimental'.

Sentimentality has meant many different things in the history of literature. For Flaubert it characterizes the quality of romantic emotion: that is, it is not so much direct or 'real', as associative –less a passion than an aspiration. Thus Henry's feelings for his mistress, his actions, his surroundings are stimulated as much by his associations with the words adultery, adventure and Paris as by the things themselves. And Flaubert notes the same tendency in Jules:

> What made one sorry for him was that he did not know how to distinguish between what is and what should be; he was always suffering from the lack of something, he was perpetually expecting something indefinable which never arrived.
> (Ibid., III, 101)

This might be considered a very ordinary state of affairs, but Flaubert's conception of it is distinctive. The very idea of a 'sentimental education' is based on an assumption that every interest, activity and accomplishment is essentially sentimental; if not actually inspired by love, it follows the same pattern of feeling and its value is emotional. Flaubert's realism aimed at analysing this romantic psychology and thus dispelling the illusions of feeling as unreal. His analysis of character is dominated by his concept of the role played by sentimental ideas. The whole spiritual energy of man seemed to him to be devoted to the vain pursuit of love, beauty and happiness. Man develops a 'sentimental' attachment for certain people, things and places, which appear to promise that indefinable something that he desires. The attachment is sentimental because the feeling and the reality do not correspond to one another, as time invariably shows. But until time has taught its lesson, both heart and mind are at the mercy of their illusions which sentimentalize the world.

The artistic difficulty lay in the fact that, so long as Flaubert tried to realize his idea with the help of a hero, he had to go along with his hero's illusions until he had learnt his lesson. Thus while Flaubert is tracing all the stages of Henry's romantic experiences, he writes sentimentally–to the full extent of his hero's feeling. Further, when the romantic feeling has burnt itself out, there is nothing left, and the hero ceases to have the emotional integrity or interest of a hero. And at this point reality itself becomes uninteresting, because it lacks the association with sentiment. Henry himself is made to realize this dilemma towards the close of the novel. Thoroughly disillusioned, his love exhausted, he is faced with an impossible alternative: not to take it seriously, which is to accept existence at the unpoetic evaluation of the bourgeois mentality he spurns, or, to recognize the eternal nothingness of life's illusions, which leaves him nothing to live for. Henry seems to get over it and becomes a non-entity; Jules evidently chose the second possibility, as Flaubert explains at the moment when his second hero thinks he is in love:

> Was he in love? He doubted it himself later when he had lived for so long an ideal life of the imagination, in the midst of celestial loves and impossible feelings, and came to deny beauty because he had loved it too much and to laugh at all the passions because of the force with which he had studied them. But at this time he was still serious about life with all its illusions, and had not tried to measure his love against the scale of the infinite: a sinister mania which disgusts us with the greatest things and makes us old too early.
>
> (Ibid., III, 100)

So Henry stops believing in love, and Jules stops believing in life; the two terms are wrenched apart and the novel ends. It ends with a kind of survey of material for its possible continuance, but the sentimental liaison between reality and feeling has been broken, and there is no artistic incentive left to sustain the fiction. Flaubert had not yet discovered how to detach himself from the sentimental disintegration of his hero and integrate his material on a 'purely' artistic basis.

The final version of the second *L'Education sentimentale* (1870), though it bears little external similarity to the first, illustrates by contrast Flaubert's achievement of artistic detachment. Only the difficulty involved in the convention of a romantic hero survived and caused Flaubert some uneasiness lest the novel fail by the failure of his new pupil, Frédéric Moreau. Flaubert interpreted the central weakness of the first version as a lack of causality in the lives of his heroes. The book had been, he said, 'an attempt to fuse the two sides of my nature', by which he meant the lyrical and the realistic. The question of causality

25

was inevitably a major issue, because each side established a different claim on it. Feeling claimed a heroic determination, while reality exposed a casual helplessness. Flaubert now went to such lengths to stress the objective concomitants to Frédéric's most indeterminate feelings, that he fell into the reverse error from his earlier lyrical extravagance; he characterized the error by saying that 'the background devours the foreground'.

Frédéric Moreau and his friends are in danger of becoming mere historical representatives of the various elements which make up the period 1840–1848; their reactions may be satisfactorily explained in terms of the political, artistic or commercial interests of the time. But the action of the novel as a whole betrays the strain of two unreconciled tendencies: Flaubert's desire to integrate his material 'purely objectively', and his concessions to the subjective integrity of his characters. George Sand located the weakness of the novel in 'the absence of any interaction between the characters'. This criticism cannot be taken quite literally; there is both action and interaction, but the two things do not fit together properly. The main theme of the action, which centres around Frédéric's love for Mme. Arnoux, is never fully realized. This is partly because it is an essentially unrealisable passion; when Frédéric first sees her, his 'desire for physical possession disappeared before a profounder longing, in an afflicting curiosity which knew no bounds'. From the start it is a sentimental experience. But the action remains unrealized also on artistic grounds for Flaubert wishes to expose this experience as it is in reality. And here he sees it as a complex of interactions between things and people and events, which inevitably end in disillusion, not because Frédéric 'fails', but because this is how reality is: indifferent to human illusions of feeling. Flaubert has denied his hero the power of effective motivation, but it is not clear whether this is a flaw of character, a weakness in characterisation, or a genuine insight into the really impersonal movement of things. The indeed ambiguous nature of reality is not rendered with complete aesthetic clarity, but interferes with the artistic effectiveness of the novel. There is a suggestion throughout of two planes that never meet, which gives to Frédéric and his friends an appearance of weak incompetence always below the level of their fate.

The artistic integration of the novel is based on a perpetual contrast between feeling and reality. The opening chapters build up a subtle complex of sentiment between the poles of Frédéric's ambition and his mother's expectation, Deslaurier's enthusiasitc plans and Frédéric's love-sick idleness, Mme Arnoux's perfection and her husband's brash flirtatiousness, Frédéric's idealistic notion of the Parisian *monde* and the tough mentality of bourgeois self-advancement, between all the dreams of love and hope and the cynical practices of commerce in the world. The constant pole of feeling is symbolized in Mme. Arnoux; Frédéric 'was in love with everything connected with Mme. Arnoux, her furniture, her servants, her house, her street'–indeed with Paris itself. Everything in Frédéric's life, from his interest in art to his interest in politics, from his affair with Rosanette to his forsaking of the wealthy widow Dambreuse at the auction of the Arnoux property 'for the sake of Mme. Arnoux', is characterized as a sentimental experience. Frédéric's sentimental response supplies the artistic interest for Flaubert's realistic picture of Parisian society.

Proust likened the style of *L'Education sentimentale* to 'the 'monotonous, perpetual movement of a moving staircase'. Things, he observed, have as much life as men, and what would conventionally have been action turns into a uniform aesthetic impression. Frédéric's feelings are merely associated with the larger movement of things of which he is a part; at no time is the 'action' associated directly with his point of view and in several scenes he might just as well not be there at all. The end is reached because time runs out on him: a fact which Mme. Arnoux acknowledges when she leaves Frédéric for the last time with a lock of her white hair–'and that was all'.

In concluding the novel Flaubert betrayed the uneasy compromise he had been making all along between his stylistic detachment and his obligations to his hero. He had to wind up the themes he had introduced into his hero's life, and from Frédéric's point of view; at the same time he had to maintain towards the expiry of Frédéric's feelings the stylistic attitude of pure indifference proper to realism. Flaubert resolved this dilemma by administering a series of sentimental shocks to which Frédéric has no further power of response. It is doubtful whether the scenes which dispose of M. Roque and his daughter, Dussardier and Sénécal, Rosanette, Mme. Dambreuse and Mme. Arnoux, and last of all the two friends, Deslauriers and Frédéric, are examples of pure realism or overstrained sentiment. The closing chapter which dispassionately represents Frédéric and Deslauriers talking over old times like men of the world, and leaves them recalling as 'the best time we ever had' how they were once humiliatingly laughed out of a brothel, makes a last, too obvious, contrast with their 'dreams of love' and their

27

'dreams of power'. This kind of contrast lies at the core of Flaubert's artistic conceptions, but it is always in danger of falling into bathos.

Critics of Flaubert have suggested that there is a biographical explanation of why he made some concession to feeling in *L'Education sentimentale*. Mme. Arnoux, who alone is spared realistic analysis and keeps Frédéric in the role of a romantic hero where she is concerned, has been identified with Mme. Schlésinger for whom Flaubert once conceived a youthful passion. He always looked back on 'the old days', as he later wrote to her, 'as though they were bathed in a golden mist'; and he believed, as Frédéric might have done, that 'what little of value still remains to me, comes from that time'. The explanation seems likely, and would perhaps account for the lengths to which Flaubert went to submerge this feeling in the drift of a historical narrative. Certainly the novel lacks the power of *Madame Bovary*, where the sentimental action merges exactly with the objective analysis of events.

The chronology of Flaubert's work has been broken for the sake of the comparison between the two versions of *L'Education sentimentale*. It may be permissible to disregard it further, in order to reserve *Madame Bovary*, *Bouvard et Pécuchet* and *Un Cœur simple* for special consideration as the finest accomplishments of Flaubert's realism and deal briefly here with his other deviations from it.

It was typical of Flaubert's attitude towards his art that, after expending so much labour on historical research and praising the muse of scientific observation, he should complain of the tedium in writing so unpoetic a work as *L'Education sentimentale*. He condemned it as 'a series of analyses and mediocre gossip'; bourgeois society was unfit for poetry, and he vowed to abandon it for his everlasting dream of the beautiful. He had experienced a similar reaction after completing *Madame Bovary*, and the two works which were intended to satisfy this longing were *Salammbô* (1863) and *La Tentation de St. Antoine* (1874). In *Salammbô* he turned to Antiquity and the East to discover a subject full of passion and plastic beauty. But his demon pursued him into the romantic distance of Carthage, which for Flaubert carried a wealth of lyrical associations, for the Orient was his *vie antérieure*, his escape from contemporary France; and it transformed even this ideal subject so thoroughly into an impersonal and artistically passionless object that the novel has the quality less of a Romantic than a Parnassian work of literature. Flaubert's lyrical enthusiasm expended itself in material research until he yawned. His poetic dreams, inspired by a 'disgust at modern life', were broken by his inability to have any real feeling for his historical characters; even while he was travelling in the East he had yearned again for France. 'One must create through the medium of the beautiful something that is nevertheless living and true', he wrote in a prefatory invocation. It was the same problem that he had encountered in *Madame Bovary*, only put the other way about. There he had tried to create through the medium of the living and true something that would nevertheless be beautiful. Flaubert summed up the difficulty when he declared his intention as having been: 'to fix a mirage by applying to Antiquity the methods of the modern novel'.

The paradox of 'fixing a mirage' reveals again the inescapable fatality of Flaubert's realism, which had oppressed his youth and 'extended itself over the whole universe', discovering everywhere man's fatal and futile illusions. His art, he said, was like the sun which 'puts gold on the dungheap'; but its searching light also made life appear corrupt and worthless, and turned even the glories of Antiquity into a mirage of spiritual nothingness. The figure is apt, for *Salammbô* was written in every sense under the influence of the sun. It is the dominating symbol of the book, a symbol of the intense plastic beauty of the East; but the intensity of its light and heat did not inspire Flaubert with a noble vision of life or any warmth of sympathetic feeling. It seemed rather to illumine in the dying carcass of Carthage a ghastly, but quite unmoving, spectacle of decay, and to reveal the heroism of the past corrupt with cruelty and superstition, the purity of divine Salammbô tainted with erotic desire, and the sanctity of religious belief divided between blind fanaticism and suicidal disillusion. The love-death of both the hero and the martyr achieves a climax that is less glorious than orgiastic.

The ambiguous conclusion reflects a questionable quality in Flaubert's artistic concept. He had hoped to portray this decadent corruption as poetry, and this raised again all the old difficulties of form and style. The form of the novel is heroic, and the hero is the very reverse of the sentimental modern man. The style of the novel is poetic, in the romantic sense that it escapes from the contemporary bourgeois world into the exotic and colourful past. The problem was to create through this medium of the beautiful something that would nevertheless be living and true. His idea of vitality and truth demanded that his hero be realized as an embodiment of fanatical energy; while his idea of beauty, particularly of Oriental beauty, was

29

inspired by a 'conviction of the nothingness of man'. So that in fact Flaubert reduces the ideal of epic heroism to shambles, at the same time that he tries to realize all the imaginative value of that poetic ideal by sheer beauty of style.

La Tentation de St. Antoine reveals essentially the same kind of situation much more directly; indeed, more than any other of his mature works, it gives something like spontaneous expression to the central problem of his art. Again a striking ambiguity is found in the conclusion of the book. In the earlier versions St. Antony is released from his night of temptations after he has heard the last pronouncement of the devil which implies that he will never escape from these spiritual nightmares: because, the devil says, St. Antony perversely loves the pleasure he derives from his self-inflicted martyrdom, it is his *only source* of spiritual experience. In the last version Flaubert carries the process one stage further, and has St. Antony conclude his spiritual labours by falling to the ground and embracing the earth in a frenzied acknowledgement that there is only 'Matter, nothing but matter!' At this moment the sun rises and, looking into it, he is vouchsafed a beatific vision.

And again the ambiguity at the close sums up a weakness that runs through the work as a whole. *La Tentation de St. Antoine* is written in the form of an allegorical drama–after the model perhaps of the puppet shows on the subject which Flaubert had seen in his youth. But both the allegory and the drama seem to have been to him mere formalities, virtually 'empty' forms as far as their real coherence or significance goes. Allegory, after all, is a very strict literary form, in which the imaginative interest is carefully matched against a framework of intellectual concepts. Flaubert drew his concepts from a wide range of philosophical and historical reading; but his imaginative realization of them is extremely vague and romantic: life is picturesque but evil, death is an illusion, the antique gods are in their last agony, all values are relative and truth is incommensurable with existence. And the drama amounts to no more than an extension of Flaubert's earlier crude contrast between a belief in a spiritually rewarding truth and the empirical evidence to the contrary. The poetic presentation of the material in itself, however, is far from crude; and Flaubert defended the style as being alone important, against the adverse criticism of his friends who saw only the insubstantial and incoherent form of the work. When, therefore, the dramatically conventional end is reached, it is not only ambiguous but artistically unimportant, just as the allegorical and dramatic significance of the various temptations has been quite inconsequential. The interest lies throughout in the realization of St. Antony's experiences as poetry, without regard for their 'real' meaning. It comes close to discovering the poetry, not of evil (for the forces of evil are better organized than the rabble of St. Antony's nightly visitors, and reflect a more substantial order of good), but of spiritual meaninglessness.

The theme of temptation certainly meant something to Flaubert, however, and he twice rewrote the work; it was, he said, 'the work of my whole life', and the only one he ever created with any spontaneous ease or satisfaction. For once he let himself go and satisfied his longing for the beautiful with a subject where the poetry of style could be matched by a plastic beauty in the material. The overall theme disposed of the romantic predicament–that the imaginative importance of all these feelings should be essentially unreal. To realize them as tempting illusions was a way of feeling them that corresponded exactly to Flaubert's experience. Surely this was the perfect theme for his art? But the problem was not to be solved so easily. Flaubert found himself again in the paradoxical position of trying to realize a purely *poetic* value in ideas while denying their *real* value. With the result that the poetry, sensuous, colourful, passionate, amounts to an aimless flight of the imagination through the unreal realms of the spirit. The shock of finding that the original version of *La Tentation* was unacceptable in the judgement of Bouilhet and Du Camp made Flaubert conscious of his true literary obligations as a realist: not to escape from the problem but to discover a coherent basis of stylistic rapprochement between his ideas and reality.

This lack of rapprochement was precisely what Du Camp objected to in *La Tentation*. 'You have made an angle,' he said, 'the two lines of which diverge to such an extent that one loses sight of them altogether'. There is indeed no point of contact between St. Antony and his visions; no conflict is possible because he and they represent two entirely different worlds. They are so divided that it is as doubtful whether he has any subjective integrity to preserve as whether they have any objective validity to assert. The problem could not be resolved in any terms of lyrical feeling because it concerned, not a battle between the saint and the devil, but Flaubert's battle with the 'higher fatality' of realism, which put the ideals of feeling to flight as mere illusion.

The distressing formlessness of vision in *La Tentation* exhibits the broken and unresolved relationship between truth and

31

reality. Reality is suddenly invaded by a kind of positivist nightmare of conflicting truths and dying values, with which St. Antony is plagued and bewildered. And yet he still believes in a redeeming vision of truth, sustained by the hope which Flaubert spoke of in his letters, that one day, from the mountain top of art and science, humanity will 'glimpse a state of soul far superior to life, beside which glory and even happiness count for nothing'. Flaubert knew—what he later considered to be a weakness of *La Tentation*—that he had simply identified himself with his saint on the mountain, in order to survey the lost countries of poetry. His review of them might be read as an artist's martyrology, which recalls everything from the voluptuous luxury of the Queen of Sheba to the vainglories of sophistry.

Does the book then represent a weakness, a lyrical exception which Flaubert was always shy about, an artistic failure? Whatever must be the verdict by the ultimate canons of literary judgement, *La Tentation de St. Antoine* represents besides the lyrical aspect of Flaubert's dedication to realism. St. Antony's profoundest temptation, which questioned the motives of his belief, might be referred to Flaubert's own belief, despite all appearances to the contrary, 'with nothing to keep me going but a kind of perpetual fury . . . that I do what is good and am in the right'. Was his rejection of 'the glory and even the happiness' of the imagination for the sake of a real truth, or merely a state of self-induced fanaticism which finds an ultimate satisfaction in pain and calls it ideal? What if his self-chastisement provoked this vision of spiritual disintegration, and his detached acceptance of this meaningless progress of historical fatality were itself the last form of nihilism? The devil tried to make St. Antony believe that he could not exist apart from the the world he had rejected, that God was an infinity that rendered his finite individuality meaningless, that there was nothing beyond the equivocal alternation of pleasure and pain within the experience of temptation itself. These are the very details of Flaubert's experience as a writer. He likened himself to an ascetic who was suffering a martyrdom of life through his aspiration towards the beautiful; and yet he seemed to inflict on himself with a perverse pleasure the very pain he would transcend. His 'pangs of style' found their figurative equivalent in the torment of St. Antony; and the anguish which Flaubert felt in realising his conception of *Madame Bovary* and *Bouvard et Pécuchet* can be compared with the saint's endurance of his tempting visions for the sake of a 'higher' reality. Only the doubt remains; for the light of his redeeming style shines in the end on an act of what appears to be spiritual annihilation in 'la matière, rien que la matière!'

III

The now established fame of *Madame Bovary*, which suggests that the novel's power is both clear and universal, contrasts with the difficulty encountered by any critical attempt to define it. The materials of the story offer no distinctive definition; rather is it astonishing that such an ordinary story can have been presented so powerfully. This forces criticism to consider those elusive qualities of style and form, which are always so awkward to discuss with regard to fiction. A brief digression may therefore be allowed, in order to sketch the main lines that distinguish the novel as a genre and thus give some points of reference by which to measure Flaubert's achievement.

Although the novel appears to have no very precise form, it constitutes nevertheless an obvious and unmistakable genre. And even if it is argued that whatever recognizable forms it has taken derive originally from drama or epic, these are still executed in a new way; they possess a novel form of interest by appearing, as it were, in a different dimension. The simplest analogy is with the discovery of perspective in painting. The solidity and depth of objects had been represented earlier; realistic perspective sprang from a changed idea of the real, whereby the focus of personal vision is itself represented to show the way in which things 'really' exist. In the novel this added dimension, which is the distinctive feature of the genre, is likewise found in the author's personal understanding of things. The art of description views everything through the eyes and mind of the novelist. Variously modified and even disguised for effect, this is the original medium in which he writes, and which provides the new 'realism' peculiar to fiction.

Dependent, however, on mere prose description, the novel has also been one of the least symbolic forms of literature. Again the point is not easy to define, though the basic fact is obvious: the novelist, inheriting a sense of dramatic, poetic and epic values, interprets them descriptively, instead of expressing them directly as drama, poetry or epic. The origins of these older genres have been traced back to ritual and myth; and they are symbolic in the sense that they create an ideal image which embodies both the intuited significance of a thing and the real substance of a thing. To explain this ideal the language of

33

aesthetics has invented terms like 'concrete-universal', or the concept that the poetic arts are essentially 'metaphorical'. Above all, these genres are uni-form; their lines are formed to produce an identity of meaning and fact–a symbolic reality where it is not doubted, for instance, that gods may mix with men, or heroes declame in verse, or metaphors are true. Indeed the existence of beautiful art has recurrently bequeathed the illusion of a really beautiful existence for later generations to yearn after. And it is perhaps interesting to note that the epithets 'poetic', 'dramatic' and 'epic' are often attributed to events that are felt actually to possess real aesthetic qualities. The word 'fiction', on the other hand, immediately suggests a contrast with 'fact'. It is possible to distinguish between a novel's truth to life and the artistry of its execution, between a description of beautiful things and a beautiful description of things; or rather, all such terms acquire a double meaning from the addition of another dimension in realistic prose. For fiction is multiform and sees another side to fact, which reveals an essential difference between the mere surface of events and the depth of their significance. Thus the novelist may describe an epic story, or a dramatic interplay of character, or poetic beauties of scene and sentiment, and most likely all these things, but every line of his description points to the direction of his own thought and relates the aesthetic qualities of the real to the perspective of his conscious understanding. His view of life may seem more real perhaps, because his appeal to a personal point of view gives his reader a sense of being 'in the picture'; but his prose account of reality is at the same time less artistic. From the outset fiction lacks the symbolic stature of the older genres, a fact that is reflected in the *mock* heroic and *mock* epic style of three of the first great European novels, *Don Quixote*, *Gargantua et Pantagruel* and *Tom Jones*.

The novel soon left behind ironical memories of the epic to explore its own potentialities. It learnt from the comedy of manners in the theatre to see man as a figure in society and to portray the social values of his existence. It kept pace with the related genres of biography and history in its understanding of the development of character against a background of time. Above all the novel was uniquely capable of bringing out the specifically subjective nature of thought and feeling; and with the Romantic intensification of 'inner' sensitivity to the 'outer' world it became the greatest genre of the century. The only serious difficulty lay in the preservation of some formal unity. Ever greater demands were made on the understanding of the

34

novelist as the conventional sense of dramatic and poetic truths gave way to a more realistic view of the world. The challenge was fully answered in the moral insight of a Tolstoy or the social insight of a Balzac. But the further progress of realism, which had set out by discovering how to make the true value of things more real than before, appears to end in the work of Proust and Joyce by having the reverse effect. They have written works of epic proportions; but these are epics, not of the real, but of the mind. And the terms are almost mutually exclusive. As studies in consciousness, *Ulysses* and *A la recherche du temps perdu* have been justly praised for their profundity of intellectual significance; but as descriptions of 'reality' they appear as distorted, fragmentary stories of triviality and insignificance. Even the conventional form of a hero and a plot, or simple narrative continuity, which survived for so long in fiction to impose some objective unity on its explorations, is virtually abandoned and replaced by a purely spiritual structure of meaning.

Flaubert's genius inevitably fell foul of the inherent conditions and tendencies of realistic fiction; in his hands they grew into serious problems and contradictions. For he detested real life and praised art as though it were some kind of transcendent negation; he wished to make his style a symbol of beauty and truth, and he despised the prosaic. The social aspect of human existence filled him with disgust, and the early version of *L'Education sentimentale* had shown already what time does for the illusions of heroic character. Above all he denied the illusions of feeling and the value which the world seems to acquire from the perspective of self-conscious experience: that foolish egocentricity that Flaubert blamed for having finally created even God in the image of man. To describe this illusion in realistic prose, and yet to make his style superior to all that he reckoned prosaic or illusory, meant that description was intended to carry a new (and seemingly self-defeating) significance. Though *Madame Bovary* is accepted as the masterpiece of realist writing, he personally declared that 'it was in hatred of realism that I undertook this book'; and though the story is one of romantic love, it is a denial of lyricism—that 'cancer of lyricism' with which he felt he had himself been consumed. It is understandable that Baudelaire should have wondered of this novel, born out of such paradoxical circumstances, whether it had not been written for a wager.

Flaubert had, in fact, been prompted to attempt it by the shock of finding that *La Tentation de St. Antoine*, which he had hoped would be a lyrical masterpiece, was condemned by his friends as a failure. He later commented that the piece lacked any 'parallelism between the facts and the ideas'. Though ostensibly working on a drama, Flaubert had already encountered the main problem of realism, a problem that seemed by its nature to be embedded in the structure of fiction. Could the symbolic values of poetry have any place in a genre founded on a realisation of the difference between *objective* facts and *subjective* ideas? It was, ultimately, the problem of how to write poetry in an age of prose, and Flaubert undertook to solve it in the prosaic medium of the realistic novel.

How far he has been successful cannot be finally decided; the most that can be done is to point out some of the changes in the style and form of fiction which his intention produced. With regard, then, to the style, it seems at first glance that Flaubert's innovations amount to little more than nuances of expression. But these nuances are unusually 'telling'. Fine shades of feeling and thought are usually the minor products of a clearly defined sense of major differences. In *Madame Bovary* the crux of the action lies in the contrast between Emma's sentimental illusions and the plain facts of reality. The contrast would seem to be clear enough; but it presented Flaubert with a complicated problem of style. For he did not believe that any spiritual perspective *really* exists to distinguish significantly between them; emotions and ideas were to be treated as mere facts in the same way as everything else. He asserted even that 'reality is no more than an illusion to be described'. It is as if the achievement of perspective had been suddenly reversed, to find man trapped by his own discovery, knowing that his new insight into the real is based on an optical illusion, yet incapable of passing beyond it; and as if Flaubert had then set his art the superhuman task of knowing reality in absolute terms. In a situation where the major dimensions of experience were held to give a false value to things, the burden fell upon style alone of revealing their true aspect and quality. Flaubert made original use of the distinction possible in fiction between *what* is described and the *way* it is described. He claimed that the essence of his art depended on finding the right 'tournure d'aspect'. And certainly the essential contrast in the novel is not between the conflicting values of fact and fancy in Emma Bovary's life, but rather between the meaning this conflict only appears to have and the negation which is transparent in Flaubert's style. His determination to discover, in a style based on such a negative idea of truth, the redeeming quality of beauty, stems from

36

the questionable romantic belief that the base matter of the real is transcended and transformed in the purely aesthetic sublimity of the idea. The nuances of Flaubert's realism reflect the ambiguity of this ideal. From one point of view they indeed represent purely artistic demands of form, clarity, order and so forth, but from another they become a matter of life and death to the soul. [1]

Needless to say, the value and importance of words was greatly increased. But this increase was paid for by a corresponding loss in the real value of human being, until the perfected phrase reads like a symbol of man's worthlessness. Flaubert's style has, in fact, that symbolic power to which he could be so sensitive in 'the most banal word' or 'gestures and tones of voice'. He restored to the language of fiction perhaps some of the symbolism of poetry; but his 'ideal image' is valued at the cost of spiritual annihilation. He was fully aware of the ambiguous quality of his ideal. Though modern aesthetics likes to find a 'reconciliation of opposites' at the core of all great art, it was a serious metaphysical problem to Flaubert whether his stylistic identity of image and idea could ever *really* reconcile the contradictions which he experienced. His style is an undoubted aesthetic accomplishment, but 'looked at from the other side' its significance detaches itself again from the reality it represents. He makes his central theme, which is romantic love, more overpoweringly real than perhaps any writer before him; but if romantic love is *in fact* such a mediocre thing caught in such petty circumstances, if it *actually* exists, not in the ideal world of poetry, but in the kind of mentality and society which Flaubert so detested, and if this is what love and longing and despair are *really* like, then the truth and beauty of style must indeed be 'detached' from such a waste of spirit.

Thus although the concept of impersonal detachment is by

[1] The subtlest aspect of Flaubert's style lies in his use of tenses. Proust claimed that its effect on the way things are seen is as great as that produced in philosophy by Kant's critiques, a comparison that assists the present definition: for Kant stated the limiting conditions contained in human perception. It is, however, extremely difficult (and perhaps impossible for a foreigner) to explain the niceties of meaning suggested by a given usage. And even Proust writes only of the impression created, in certain passages of *L'Education sentimentale*, as of the 'monotonous, perpetual movement of a moving staircase'. If a further opinion may be hazarded, it is simply that Flaubert used subtleties of tense, which do not always produce a monotonous continuity but sometimes unexpected accelerations, interruptions, and changes in the distance and duration of time, to break the illusory consequence of personal experience, in the way suggested above. A realistic account of time is one of the forms in which fiction grasps the significance of life, a significance that Flaubert wished to represent, not as real, but as an aesthetic illusion.

no means original with Flaubert, he gave it a new, indeed a crucial, importance. It meant a great deal more than just suppressing personal comment in order to let reality 'speak for itself'—a common, but particularly fallacious, interpretation with regard to a genre that, unlike the truly impersonal forms of the symbolic arts, is based on the illusion of personal omniscience. That the meaning is more subtle is suggested by Flaubert's apparently contradictory remark, 'Madame Bovary, c'est moi'; and apart from this, the number of lyrical similes and intellectual observations in the book must discredit so superficial a view of the matter. For what does it mean for a writer ever to express his *own* feelings and ideas? Even a lyric poet uses language and themes formed by prevailing modes of sensitivity. And Flaubert's ideal of impersonality, which caused him such mortification of heart and mind, was shaped by the dilemma that he saw confronting the soul of modern times. It meant sacrificing the values of personality to an impersonal ideal of truth, an ideal which virtually denied the value of existence altogether, while maintaining the validity of a kind of absolute knowledge. The fate of Emma Bovary, which seems so far removed from his own, is described in a style that symbolizes Flaubert's awareness of that ideal. His stylistic detachment subtly undermines the significance of personal experience and destroys the illusions of love, adventure, heroism—in fact, of the 'reality of poetry in life'. Flaubert's style may be objective, but it shows that the objective world has really nothing to say for itself.

Flaubert's impersonal detachment is apparent in every line he wrote, and produces an ambiguous 'contrast' between its aesthetic significance and its material context; ambiguous, because his stylistic accomplishment represents a purely aesthetic harmony, and in effect a telling discord, between the artistry and the material. And though Flaubert admired the impersonality of the older poetic genres, he knew that he emulated only the letter and not the spirit of their example. For the great authors whom he praised, impersonality had been like the exercise of a symbolic privilege; to him it resembled rather the exercise of a symbolic curse. The difference is between writers able to realize their personal sense of poetry in a universal symbol of human experience, and a realist for whom reality will no longer support the symbolic forms of poetry, and universal truth is incompatible with feeling. So that Flaubert's ideal of beauty and truth could never actually be realized—unless in a book about nothing—and he could never rid himself of the

38

doubt that he might be pursuing a chimera. In symbolizing the illusions imposed on the real by man's emotions, he could perhaps transcend the limitations of personal vision. But the virtue of stylistic detachment alone would, in itself, be likewise entirely abstract and negative. It would lack the dimension in which the spirit *really* exists–as a consequence of an ideal which makes art and reality mutually exclusive.

But 'art has got to be human', and if Flaubert was fated never to realize his unattainable ideal, he could symbolize the curse which afflicts the spirit in a world where no real poetry exists. The redeeming feature, for the human interest of the novel, if not for the dilemma of his art, is supplied ironically by the effect of his style on the actual content of his story, which Flaubert so despised. For this has all the appearance of being a story that matters, a real adventure of the soul. And when the dimension on which the life of the soul depends is destroyed by the style of its telling, an ambiguous interest attaches to the most commonplace experiences. The structure of spiritual perspective in the novel is undermined in such a way that the personal misfortunes of Emma are weighted with the 'impersonal' downfall of the whole edifice of human values. Her suffering is intensified by the destructive implications of Flaubert's realism, which break the established relationships between the spirit and the world, between individual will and the external course of events, between objective facts and subjective ideas. Two of his best, though unfortunately briefest, critics, Proust and Du Bos, have described his realism as 'hermetic' or 'lacking in air'. What is lacking is the very breathing space of the spirit, and Flaubert's art has the powerful, but questionable, effect of representing spiritual suffocation in the ethereal purity of truth.

So much for the significance of the style in *Madame Bovary*. Flaubert's further modifications in the form of the novel are easier to define. The conventional requirements of a tragic narrative, which preserve the appearance of a materially significant fiction, he took care to fulfill with unexceptionable correctness, though they are largely mere formalities as they were in *La Tentation*. They bored him, but he was scrupulous in his care, and worried whether, for instance, the action in the first half of the book did not receive an improperly small amount of attention. But, he reflected, *Madame Bovary* is rather in the nature of a biography:

The dramatic element plays little part in it, and if it is drowned in the general tone of the book, perhaps the lack

39

of harmony between the different phases with respect to their development will not be noticed; and then it seems to me that life itself is rather like that. [1]

It is thus a mere formality to consider Emma as the heroine of the novel, and obviously absurd to think of her husband or either lover as in any sense its hero. The judgement that Emma and Charles lack will cannot, therefore, be understood (by the traditional criterion of dramatic action) as a fatal flaw of character. The fatality that wrecks their lives is an inherent aspect of Flaubert's artistic intention, rather than a failure of intention in their individual personalities. Emma's fate lies in supposing herself engaged in a dramatic conflict, in a world where the possibilities and responsibilities of drama no longer exist. She is the victim less of circumstance than of feeling, and the conflict is ultimately between her perpetual aspiration and her inevitable disillusion. Her disillusion is occasioned apparently by Charles, Rodolphe and Leon, but Flaubert's style reveals the real cause in the essential unreality of her sentimental ideas–even of her sentimental disillusion. The happiness she imagines (even in death) cannot be had in reality, not because men are incompetent, deceitful or weak, but because her ideal is really no more than a projection of her own emotions, an illusion of feeling. The beautiful idealisations of romantic love turn into a case history of frustration. Frustrated by the discipline of the convent, Emma imagines poetic romances; frustrated by the loneliness of home, she marries Charles; frustrated by the mediocrity of married life, she falls in love with Leon; frustrated by his departure, she yields to Rodolphe; frustrated by his betrayal and her weariness with piety, she abandons herself completely with Leon. Such is the 'realistic' psychology of one of the greatest themes of European literature. The poetry of striving appears as a progressive exhaustion of feeling, which becomes ever more the victim of its own self-deception–until Emma, in a scene near the end, longs again for the beautiful illusions of her convent days. No wonder that Flaubert considered happiness to be a lure of the devil!

In the same way, Flaubert's use of irony must be understood in a different sense from that originally given to it by the drama. Dramatic irony is one way of phrasing a conflict between man and his environment, where he is personally deceived for a while, for the sake of heightening the contrast with his eventual reconciliation and enlightenment. For Flaubert irony was not

[1] Quoted by A. Thibaudet, *Gustave Flaubert*, p. 89, Paris 1922.

a method of intrigue, but an inevitable outcome of the creative act. For he saw the whole dramatic frame of reference which man vainly uses to express his understandings and misunderstandings, his intriguing sense of being able to come to terms with the world at all, as a sheer illusion. And thus the occasional ironies of dramatic discord become a permanent condition of his realism. The irony of the dramatist who views reality under the aspect of character which can sometimes be effectively deluded is the reverse of Flaubert's irony which sees character under the aspect of a reality that is indifferent to all man's vain delusions. And if Flaubert's irony appears sometimes to be 'theatrical', this points again to his detachment from any share in the real dramatic responsibility.

'The poetry of the adulterous wife is only true to the extent that she is at liberty in the midst of fatality' Flaubert wrote at the time when he was planning *Madame Bovary*. Man's place in the universe has always been defined by these two terms of liberty and fatality, of freedom and fate. Flaubert brought to his consideration of the problem a third term: poetry. It was for him primarily an aesthetic problem. No ethical truths, no individual heroism, no universal laws of justice, retribution or harmony offered any real basis for resolving the age-old question of man's conflict with destiny. Poetry, as Flaubert understood it, could no longer be found in any of the conventional meanings which this conflict might only appear to have; it existed, if at all, in a purely aesthetic balance between the intensity of Emma's feelings and the impersonal fatality of style. Fatality becomes, as a result, the reverse aspect, not so much of any real liberty, as of illusion; while the freedom of the soul is weighed, not so much against any really significant fate, as against the damning effects of realism. Where illusion is strongest, as with Emma and Charles, the force of fatality is most intense; where it is weakest, as with Rodolphe and Lheureux who have few illusions, it has little power to harm; with Homais and Bournisien it is merely playful. It is here that Flaubert's style introduces into what is perhaps the basic form of narrative, the conflict between the hero and his fate, that ambiguous kind of aesthetic contrast which is the distinctive feature of his work.

Some of Flaubert's contrasts are too familiar to require exposition—as, for instance, the scene at the *Comices Agricoles* where the phrases and gestures of love are matched against the banalities of civic ceremony. Others are more subtle, but no less blighting to the soul. After Rodolphe's

41

betrayal Emma is sick with despair and exhorted to religious comfort by the Abbé Bournisien. Flaubert's account of her devotions gives at once the fervour of her thoughts and their entirely transient quality as a feeling provoked by her frustration and self-pity. She has been receiving the regular visits of Bournisien, who had the habit of 'mingling religious exhortation with sly pieces of gossip in a way that she found far from unattractive'. The reader is already familiar with the priest's gross imcomprehension of Emma's distress and his unconsciously ironical mixture of worldly interests with holy doctrine. There is perhaps no more than a light strain of conventional irony in the fact that 'the mere sight of his soutane brought her a sense of comfort'. But when the narrative arrives at a more serious experience, Emma's belief that she is dying, Flaubert's description discovers profounder ironies of its own in the way it matches objective details with images of feeling.

Un jour qu'au plus fort de sa maladie elle s'était crue agonisante, elle avait demandé la communion; et, à mesure que l'on faisait dans sa chambre les préparatifs pour le sacrement, que l'on disposait en autel la commode encombrée de sirops et que Félicité semait par terre des fleurs de dahlia, Emma sentait quelque chose de fort passant sur elle, qui la débarassait de ses douleurs, de toute perception, de tout sentiment. Sa chair allégée ne pensait plus, une autre vie commençait; il lui sembla que son être, montant vers Dieu, allait s'anéantir dans cet amour comme un encens allumé qui se dissipe en vapeur[1].

The tense, which reveals Emma's error in supposing that she is dying, the slightly fanciful touch in the phrase 's'était crue agonisante' and in the dahlia blossoms, the impersonal verbs which follow the causal suggestion in 'à mesure que' to link her fallacious intimation of death with her intimation of heavenly bliss, Flaubert's favourite contrast of medicine and religion, the compounded feelings of sense and spirit in her fatal yearning for 'another life' of romantic bliss, the sensual simile of incense: these are the nuances that betray the emotional delusion in Emma's piety. The passage continues:

On aspergea d'eau bénite les draps du lit; le prêtre retira du

[1] It has seemed desirable in quoting from *Madame Bovary* and *Bouvard et Pécuchet*, where style is of primary importance, to give the passages in the original; *Madame Bovary*, Conard, Paris 1921; p. 295. An English translation is given in the Appendix.

42

saint ciboire la blanche hostie; et ce fut en défaillant d'une joie céleste qu'elle avança les lèvres pour accepter le corps du Sauveur qui se présentait. Les rideaux de son alcôve se gonflaient mollement, autour d'elle, en façon de nuées, et les rayons des deux cierges brûlant sur la commode lui parurent être des gloires éblouissantes. Alors elle laissa retomber sa tête, croyant entendre dans les espaces le chant des harpes séraphiques et apercevoir en un ciel d'azur, sur un trône d'or, au milieu des saints tenant des palmes vertes, Dieu le Père tout éclatant de majesté, et qui d'un signe faisait descendre vers la terre des anges aux ailes de flamme pour l'emporter dans leurs bras.

Perhaps the final comment on this scene was written by Flaubert himself when he described, at the close of *Un Cœur simple*, Félicité's religious vision. But even here the images of Emma's feeling make it clear that she is experiencing nothing more (or should it be less?) real than a resurgence of romantic emotion. The passage is almost sensual in the factuality of its description, and the reader's sense of the true nature of her feelings is increased by his perception that what *she* takes to be real is in fact an illusion. This kind of ambiguity is woven into the texture of *Madame Bovary* and is not confined to an occasional scene. As the narrative continues, Emma's desire 'to become a saint' becomes indistinguishably involved in all the cheap trappings of religious devotion and literature, in further emotional extravagances, in the usual banalities of her environment and, of course, in her fatal psychology of insatiable desire; until her thirst for new satisfactions takes her to the theatre in Rouen, and to the next stage in her downfall.

The overwhelming effect of Emma's death does not spring from her heroic action, nor from any grandeur or dignity in her personality, but from the emotional tension built up by Flaubert's style. Her fate is typically ambiguous, and it has often been said that money, not love, is the cause of her ruin. This oversimplifies the issue; for Romeo and Juliet are the victims of a family feud, but this makes their tragedy no less one of love. The difference is between a heroic concept of conflict between love and tragic destiny, and a descriptive realism which treats love as an endless round of frustration and delusion, reduces destiny to sordid trivialities and undermines the dignity of conflict by a subtle play of irony. Thus Emma's bid for heroic effectiveness, which for a moment seems genuine in her outburst against Rodolphe, only betrays again

43

her sentimental illusions and her suicidal exhaustion of feeling.

Each stage in her fall is matched against details which undercut its significance: her despair is brought to the level of vulgar debauch, her struggle against catastrophe thwarted by lies and indecent advances, nemesis is realized in the scandal of village gossip and tragic ecstasy experienced over a bottle of arsenic 'with the clatter of forks on plates in the next room', while her reconciliation with Charles is met with sentimental incomprehension. Her suicide commands a moment of grave importance in Homais' pretentious *Capharnaüm*, where two previous scenes had already contrasted her anguish with the petty details of village life. But the irony of these circumstances, of Justin's helpless obedience to the woman he admires as the model of *Conjugal Love*, of the arsenic which nearly got mixed with Mme. Homais' preserves, diffuses the gravity of Emma's action. The shift in literary focus from a heroine to a village doctor's wife blurs the values of the spirit to the point of illusion.

Flaubert intensifies the perverse strains of his poetic method to a degree that makes it doubtful whether reality–not to speak of art–can sustain them. There is something implausibly morbid in the timely appearance of the Blind Man, to whose infernal wretchedness Emma had once given all her money, and who comes singing a ditty of love to annihilate her with terror. And there are touches of harrowing sentimentality, as in Emma's remorse when she weeps over her own reflection in the mirror. But Flaubert soon recovers the balance of his style in the ironical detachment of the medical colloquy and the last debate between Homais and Bournisien over Emma's corpse. The list of Flaubert's ironies is endless, and it concludes with the famous scene between Rodolphe and Charles, when the husband acknowledges as a kind of death sentence the fatality which the lover had glibly used as a convenient cliché of love. Even the traditional resolution which man finds in the all-forgiving acceptance of his destiny is sacrificed to the still inexorable demands of Flaubert's realism, and reduced to the level of Charles' mediocre intelligence and Rodolphe's cheap sensitivity:

–Je ne vous en veux pas, dit-il [Charles].

Rodolphe était resté muet. Et Charles, la tête dans les deux mains, reprit d'une voix éteinte et avec l'accent résigné des douleurs infinies:

–Non, je ne vous en veux plus!

Il ajouta même un grand mot, le seul qu'il ait jamais dit:

–C'est la faute de la fatalité!

Rodolphe, qui avait conduit cette fatalité, le trouva bien
débonnaire pour un homme dans sa situation, comique même
et un peu vil.   (Ibid., p. 480)

When the celebrated prosecution of the novel arose, on the
grounds that it offended public morality and religion, it was not
difficult to establish in court that the details of Emma's religious
experiences were orthodox enough. And with regard to the
'moral' of the book, the defence begged the question by arguing
that such a realistic picture of the ruin brought about by
immorality offered a clear exhortation to virtue. For the question
is, precisely, what kind of meaning remains to moral values
in Flaubert's aesthetic analysis of life? The now familiar answer
that art has nothing to do with ethics is probably as superficial as
the legal protest against an occasional shocking description.
The novel's really shocking power is based on the unstated
implications of its realism, which to the last detail seems to bear
out a most conventional view of life, at the same time that it
makes it doubtful whether there is anything to choose between
vice and virtue.

Flaubert's narrative dwells almost continuously in *Madame
Bovary* on the more or less ambiguous meaning of experience;
the reader is repeatedly made to *feel* its emotional significance
and to *see* its annihilating triviality. Mr. Turnell has observed
that 'Flaubert had no gift for *direct* description . . . His originality
appears rather in sudden glimpses into the *moral* significance
of a person or a place . . .' [1] The comment was inspired by the
unsuccessful attempts at direct description in *L'Education sentimentale*, and the word 'sentimental' might be used to define the
dubious kind of moral significance which Flaubert perceived.
For the moral significance of things represented to him an
unreal association or projection of feeling, and it is the emotional
quality of this illusion which he symbolizes in his most effective
descriptions. *Madame Bovary* abounds in symbols and poetic
similes, and in repeated images that presage the use of *leitmotiv*
by Proust and Joyce. Trite conversations, domestic scenery,
commonplace objects, details of landscape and village life are
coloured with different shades of sentiment, some of them
notoriously purple, others carrying subtler tones of mood and
meaning. But the effect is always the same; wherever Flaubert
manages to pin down the quality of an emotion in material
terms, he lays bare another illusion of the soul for what it is:
a sentimental delusion. Reality gains at the expense of the

[1] *The Novel in France* Hamilton, London 1950; p. 295.

spirit: which is, perhaps, why the famous, factual description of the mere progress of the cab in which Leon seduces Emma so powerfully conveys the spiritual emptiness of her last bid for happiness.

Criticism has found fault with the ambiguities involved in *Madame Bovary*. Though it is the acknowledged masterpiece of realism, its elaborate use of style has caused it to be found artificial. And although the style is intended to be detached and impersonal, its purity is so stained with the sacrifice of feeling which it represents that the book has been judged overly sentimental. But these traits cannot properly be judged apart by conventional standards; they are mere indications of the profounder elements of which Flaubert has made the novel. And these elements effect a serious change in the ideas and values attaching to fiction.

IV

In the summer of 1872 Flaubert completed the third version of *La Tentation de St. Antoine*. Almost immediately he turned his attention to a work that stands in striking contrast to it: *Bouvard et Pécuchet*. It was to be his last book (though interrupted by the production of *Trois Contes*) and it remained unfinished; but it was as much a 'work of his whole life' as *La Tentation*, and was planned on the same epic scale. Although he had vowed never to return to a bourgeois subject, he came now to the most consummately bourgeois of them all: a compendious satire of two copying clerks in their search for knowledge.

The history of *Bouvard et Pécuchet* might be said to begin with the often-quoted letter that Flaubert wrote to a friend at the age of nine, suggesting that they 'write together, I my comedies, you your dreams, and as there is a lady who visits papa and who tells us silly things, I could write them down'. Flaubert's last work is a monumental collection of silly things. And his inspiration at fifty might be traced back to the impulses of scorn and disgust which inspired him at fifteen to invent *Le Garçon*, that imaginary character which he and his friends would personate in order to parody and mock the citizens of Rouen. The material he used reads like an extended version of his *Dictionnaire des idées reçues*, to which *Le Garçon* had made the first contributions and Flaubert had then added, throughout a lifetime of satirical observation, every detail of opinion and habit that characterized the bourgeois world he detested.

The fact that so much of what has gone into the making of

46

Bouvard et Pécuchet can be related directly to the attitudes and experiences of Flaubert's earlier years has sometimes exposed him to criticism for immaturity or narrowness. It is true that he remained obsessed by the same kind of problem all his life, and that even his ideal of impersonality reflects it. And in this sense there is indeed a recognisable sameness to all Flaubert's work, which never sees or says very much more than what was contained already in that first gift (or curse) of adolescent inspiration. Whether this 'could make up the *whole* vision of a man of his distinction' is a question that has disturbed even so sympathetic an admirer as Henry James. And it is not hard to understand the misgivings felt by Zola and Turgenev when they found their friend apparently turning back to the most unpromising, and at the same time uncompromising, treatment of his oldest *bête noire*. For *Bouvard et Pécuchet* was to be the 'thing itself', the drab folly of real life, made universal by its total denial, not only of the romantic spirit of poetry, but of culture itself. If Flaubert could succeed with such a subject, it would be, as he hoped, 'an artistic triumph', an unconditional victory for art without concession to any material interest in the fiction.

From the point of view of its form *Bouvard et Pécuchet* does offer something new. Indeed, Flaubert almost never wrote twice in the same form. He was not a great artist of life, like Balzac, but an artist of words; it was not life that interested him, but the artistic process as such. He claimed to have read over 1500 volumes in preparation for his last novel, but in all this abundance of material he was looking for only one thing: the essence of a particular kind of satire. He reduced these volumes to the basest usage, made his material appear all nauseatingly alike; but he won for his art possibilities of expression that are unique. Of course, the expression 'means' something too; and thus Flaubert's vision of life is also, indirectly, new. But the value of this vision can only be understood in relation to the artistic process which gave rise to it. Otherwise *Bouvard et Pécuchet* must appear as one of Flaubert's most banal books, pedantically cataloguing arbitrary instances of human silliness. Everything depends upon the artistic level at which the satire has been offered; the silliness itself is painfully obvious. [1]

[1] A fact which led Flaubert to predict, disconcertingly, that any criticism or commentary on the book would be as silly as everything else his heroes meet with, and worthy of inclusion in the *sottisier*, the encyclopaedia of absurdities with which the book was to conclude.

Bouvard et Pécuchet resembles *La Tentation de St. Antoine* in that both works appear to be perilously balanced between extraordinary success and total failure. The selection of a critical terminology is enough to determine their fate; subsequent analysis merely confirms either of two foregone conclusions. Criteria of style inevitably incline towards praise, while discussion in traditional terms of drama or fiction leads to disappointment. Both works share, besides, one particularly baffling trait. Their material content, voluminous though it is in outline, is curiously insubstantial and fleeting. Once rendered, its significance is apparently lost and, with one or two exceptions, the matter is not brought up again. Their styles are undoubtedly different; but again they share the quality of achieving their own peculiar excellence at the price of rendering the material all essentially the same. In *La Tentation* it becomes a panorama of illusions; in *Bouvard et Pécuchet* a bathetic exhibition of futility and fatuousness. In either case the style, when looked at from the point of view of someone interested in the material (as drama or fiction), seems lifeless; while the material, when viewed from the vantage point of pure style, appears more and more abstract, its interest intellectual ('somewhere in the middle between algebra and music' perhaps) and as near to that Platonic 'law of numbers' as Flaubert could ever get. He is praised for having found the *mot juste*; but the execution of aesthetic justice has the effect of transforming the material into the 'platonic' image of a thing that itself has been denied. Viewed at this level, Flaubert's sustained 'satire' against his material (which is indeed all at this one level) does begin to make more serious sense.

Bouvard et Pécuchet is satire of a new kind. Conventional forms of satire have generally implied a normative point of view, from which abnormalities appear in a satirical light. This may have been a moral standpoint, or some discreet complex of philosophical assumptions representing 'common sense'. Now Flaubert does not make altogether clear what is being satirized. As his two clerks undertake their encyclopaedic researches into every aspect of life, they are frustrated by the simplest incompetence and the most banal accidents. Taken in conjunction with the original subtitle, 'On the Want of a Method', the satire might seem to be directed merely at their small-minded inefficiency in matters of great weight. But that Flaubert should have devoted a whole volume (and six or eight years' work) to such a 'pedagogical' purpose is inconceivable. He was no such pedant–though he acknowledged an

48

appearance of pedantry as one of the pitfalls in his way. The proposed sub-title is more likely ironical, for Bouvard and Pécuchet themselves believe that all they need is the right method in order to achieve success in each new venture. One of their recurrent problems is to distinguish between conflicting authorities on method. It might also be supposed, then, that the satire is directed against the current state of knowledge, or against the folly of believing in any method that should make sense, either practical or theoretical. There are a few debatable passages where it could be argued that Flaubert is really intending to expose some art or science as absurd in itself. But his protagonists provide such a patently absurd and unfair medium in which to put truth to the test that the direct relevance of his satire becomes altogether ambiguous. If it is read as straight satire against either the ideas or the protagonists alone, it is likely to appear as silly as its expressed object–whichever this is considered to be.

Such a conclusion is not surprising in a discussion of so paradoxical a talent as Flaubert's; he himself dealt in double negatives and renounced all conclusions. This was the medium of his art, and the ambiguity of his satire relates back to his ideal of pure style. Genuine absurdities in the activities and ideas of the day are compounded with the personal idiosyncracies of Bouvard and Pécuchet in such a way that the perspective is lacking for any clear distinction to be drawn between them. There is really nothing to choose between the endless instances of nonsense in the world which Flaubert hunted down with such persistence and the senselessness of his characters' persistent struggle with them. That change in spiritual perspective which has already been referred to reaches a new, and perhaps extreme, point in *Bouvard et Pécuchet*.

A comparison with *Candide*, a work much admired by Flaubert, may help to clarify this development and define the original quality of his satire. For Voltaire also directs his satire against certain fallacious ideas, which he ridicules by exposing them to an absurdly contradictory reality. The metaphysics of optimism are displayed as an altogether unrealistic way of thinking–in fact, the reality which Voltaire portrays apparently defies the possibility of any philosophical comprehension; it begins to resemble rather the nightmare of a madman. With the important difference, however, that this nightmare is described with the most serene intellectual poise. Its absurdities are related with perfect rationality, and their horror has the reassuring quality of a sound argument. It is characteristic of Voltaire that

49

he can treat the most irrational state of affairs with such a confident display of reason. His doubt of metaphysics as a realistic way of thinking is not accompanied by any real metaphysical doubt about the effectiveness of rational thought. The senselessness of the world is set in an entirely objective context and construed in a way that shows very clearly what sense should be. Voltaire's realism is based on a rational perspective which allows the validity of an idea to be measured against its object.

Flaubert, on the other hand, ridicules Bouvard and Pécuchet's entire efforts to realize the validity of any idea at all. His realism measures the psychological reality of ideas, and the context in which they are experienced is the two clerks' own very limited horizon. Objectively speaking, they really experience nothing at all by comparison with the adventures that befall Candide. He travels the world in order to discipline his mind in the hard lesson of its absurdities; they explore the absurd resources of their mind in the quite futile attempt to know something of the world. To show the absurdity of an idea, Voltaire points to the facts of his hero's experience, while Flaubert points to the way his would-be heroes in fact experience it. Voltaire's satire is in the interests of a more real effectiveness of the mind in its dealings with reality, whereas Flaubert satirizes the real ineffectiveness of the mind as it is in reality. Thus the comparison ultimately arrives at the difference between what each writer thought of as real. The real absurdities of Voltaire's universe are, or should be, dissociated from the integrity of the rational mind. Realism meant to him the right exercise of reason, which he confidently expected to maintain a spiritually valid standard of truth in a universe where metaphysics are a waste of time. Flaubert's realism is more thorough-going, to the point of recognising that it amounted to meta-physical nihilism. Such an abstract standard of truth as realism demanded really left nothing to believe in. He experienced these demands with none of Voltaire's moral confidence in the rightness of reason, but rather with an intense moral despair; to him realism meant a denial of the spirit, an irrational impulse, repulsive yet compelling, to realize this rational creature, man, as a worthless *petit crapaud*. Indeed, what was real to him seems virtually to have been defined by instances of man's mental helplessness.

This difference affects every aspect of each author's work, affects even Flaubert's characterisation of Voltaire as a crusader and himself as a martyr. Above all it accounts for the different perspective in which everything appears in their satire. For Flaubert reality is not that unambiguously objective 'fact' which it was for Voltaire; nor do ideas present themselves with the same independent rationality. This convenient perspective of rational thought is submerged in the reality embodied by the experiences of Bouvard and Pécuchet. Here the absurdity of the world and the absurdity of ideas cannot be measured against anything more reliably real than their own absurdity of mind. There is only one external standpoint, and that is the pure artistry with which Flaubert, quite impersonally, depicts this ambiguous state of affairs.

The difference is reflected again in the indomitable candour of Voltaire's hero and the invincible simple-mindedness of Bouvard and Pécuchet; for the former there is hope, for the latter none. Flaubert's two clerks even make Voltaire's stoic assurance seem very much a thing of the past. Can we 'cultivate our garden' with much success when the metaphysics of an ordered universe have been exploded? It is precisely their garden which is the scene of Bouvard and Pécuchet's disastrous undertakings—and it defies cultivation. They encounter endless failure, confusion and senselessness, no matter what they cultivate; their researches get nowhere, their knowledge means nothing, their experiments do not work, even their plants will not grow. Viewed satirically, this is how the world appears when it is utterly divested of all metaphysical realities, when 'ideas are treated as facts and beliefs dissected like organisms'. For when the metaphysical reality of ideas and beliefs is denied, they have nothing to sustain them—except perhaps an inexplicable act of will that springs obstinately from man's inner nature despite all evidence of its futility. It is just such a demonstration of perverse will-power that distinguishes Flaubert's copying clerks. Even their profession is symbolic: to copy the pattern of a culture that is no longer real. Moreover their spiritual adventure takes place after their retirement from practical 'business' life, in the seclusion of their ineffectual estate. And symbolically this is the fitting place of solitary confinement for the condemned spirit, cut off from any effective contact with the real world and left to consume itself by sheer force of its own foolish intensity.

Thus the ambiguity of the satire in *Bouvard et Pécuchet* does not mean that the satire is crude. The fact that it is impossible to distinguish between the foolishness of the ideas the two clerks deal with, and the foolishness of their dealings with them, lies at the centre of Flaubert's inspiration. This *is* the fate of ideas in an utterly 'realistic' setting. When their metaphysical validity is lost, their objective substance becomes indistinguishably mixed up with all the subjective inadequacies, limitations and vicissitudes of human personality and experience. Like a corrosive acid, Bouvard's and Pécuchet's will to experience every aspect of civilised life eats through the material of civilisation at an alarming speed, compounding with it to form a worthless substance. No wonder that Flaubert strove so hard (and with such doubts at what he called his own 'rage d'user les choses') to rescue the truth of art from this dilemma, and to rediscover an objective vision that would be absolutely impersonal.

The apparently perverse exaggeration of human folly in *Bouvard et Pécuchet* concerns, therefore, a profounder problem than mere *bêtise* as such. The madness of mankind lacked method at a level which could turn a satirical perception of trivial foolishness into a lifelong obsession with something that seemed to Flaubert to endanger the possibility of art. That something was the kind of reality which such trivialities typified; they were symbols to Flaubert of a world that is meaningless, not in a local but in an absolute sense. For where the metaphysical reality of ideas and beliefs is doubted, the aesthetic reality of beauty ('the plastic beauty of the passions, etc.') is also put in doubt. Indeed, art is particularly sensitive to the problem, for nowhere is the suggestion more paralysing to the spirit that an idea is without real validity, an expression only of subjective feeling, a fact of overwrought personality, a disturbance of the organism. Mallarmé's answer was to say that 'poetry is not written with ideas, but with words'–a solution that greatly tempted Flaubert, but which is scarcely applicable to fiction whatever its success in poetry. For fiction is indissolubly linked with the real life of things; its medium is realistic description. And thus Flaubert could not help seeing the problem of words 'from the other side'. He knew that an idea must have died before it could become a pure matter of words; and in *Bouvard et Pécuchet* his style incurs, in fact, the death of innumerable ideas. To kill them required, from the point of view of the fiction, a grotesque degree of resourcefulness in the characterisation of lethal imbecility; but it enabled Flaubert to come to grips with his problem.

It was a problem, then, concerning the method of art within the conditions imposed by realism, a problem not so much of the things that are looked at as of the way they are looked at. To Flaubert realism meant seeing life itself, the simple fact of human experience, in a kind of lifeless perspective which made it quite devoid of real significance. Insignificance, therefore, became the ostensibly 'real' subject of his last satire–with the result that, taken at face value, the satire seems trivial. The dilemma is apparent: if satire implies some ultimate measure of significance in the world, how could Flaubert write a significant satire and still be true to his uncompromising experience of realism? The only solution was to transform this experience itself into satire–to represent absurdity by seeing it in the context, not of a reality in which sense can be distinguished from folly, but of a reality in which it cannot, an 'invincible' reality that lacks the marks of spiritual distinction. The most rigorous realism, the process whereby ideas die and the illusory perspective of a true relationship between the spirit and the world is destroyed, should be rendered in itself as a work of art. Thus the 'really' insignificant satire of character and ideas in *Bouvard et Pécuchet* should perhaps be read as a satirical exhibition of realism, as the art which renders life insignificant.

In no work of Flaubert's is the separation of form and content more striking. The content of his satirical observations is scarcely original or profound; it is the way in which the trite superficiality of events is realized that is alone important. It cannot be denied that sometimes this seems implausibly unfair to life, particularly to the life of ideas. But the point does not lie in judging whether the instances of nonsense which Flaubert satirizes are distorted or unrepresentative; it lies in his discovery of a style which invalidates any spiritual criterion of 'true' representation. The world may be able to do better than Bouvard and Pécuchet; but can any real improvement withstand the kind of satirical destruction of meaning in reality which Flaubert's realism effects?

Bouvard et Pécuchet is, so to speak, a book about why realistic art is no longer possible, satirizing (where *La Tentation* had lyricized) the death of any really significant vision of the world –satirizing, in effect, itself. St. Antony knew the great ideas of the spirit to be no more than tempting illusions; Bouvard and Pécuchet discover them at the other end of the scale–as hardened facts in a reality where their meaning is lost, like relics or fossils with inadequate museum tags. The 'real' content of the novel, what at first sight looks like a distorted attempt at realistic satire, was to have reached the final stage of spiritual annihilation in the conclusion Flaubert never wrote. For he planned to have his two dispirited clerks settle down, at the end of their devastating career, to copy out his own collection

53

of *bêtises*–the very source from which he had drawn the material for the book! This, surely, is the ultimate stroke of satire, against his own novel and the labour of realism–if, indeed, satire is still the right word.

In no other work of Flaubert's is it so true that the effectiveness of style is based purely on the abstract possibilities of 'accomplished execution'. This does not mean that the syntax has simply been varied to make the nullities and dullities of the subject matter less tedious reading. The style had to accomplish in detail what the form undertook in general: to render everything in Bouvard and Pécuchet's experience *as* satire–their successes as well as their failures, their feelings and ideas as well as their actions and circumstances, their integrity and their imbecility, even, finally, their 'true' perception of the folly of it all. A few examples may be quoted at random to illustrate Flaubert's method.

> Les deux archéologues furent très pénauds, balbutièrent. L'objet en question n'était plus d'usage.
> N'importe! ils devaient le rendre.
> Sans doute! Mais, au moins, qu'on leur permît de faire venir un peintre pour le dessiner.
> –Soit, messieurs.
> –Entre nous, n'est-ce pas? dit Bouvard, sous le sceau de la confession!

> Quelle émotion quand s'arrêta devant leur grille la voiture de M. de Faverges! Il n'avait qu'un mot à dire. Voici la chose:

> Et, de l'insouciance des dates, ils passèrent au dédain des faits. Ce qu'il y a d'important, c'est la philosophie de l'histoire! Bouvard ne put achever le célèbre discours de Bossuet.
> –L'aigle de Meaux est un farceur! Il oublie la Chine, les Indes et l'Amérique . . . [1]

These brief extracts may be adequate to show that what Flaubert's style achieves, firstly, is an unusual degree of factuality. This is not so simple as the uncomplicated brevity of so many of the paragraphs might suggest. Each fact is isolated in turn, with sufficient detachment from the next to emphasize the absence of any real perspective between one kind of fact

[1] *Bouvard et Pécuchet*: Conard, Paris, 1923; pp. 139, 134, 153. For translation see Appendix.

and another. And since facts presented all from the same point of view inevitably fall into some kind of perspective and assume a real meaning as a whole, this has required a constant interruption of stylistic continuity, by means of every change in tense, person, subject, tone, direct and reported speech, and whatever other device of syntax and vocabulary Flaubert could muster. That is why virtually every phrase set him a new problem in expression: how to turn it aesthetically to bring out its essential sameness as a fact. The problem has that paradoxical and self-defeating quality which characterizes Flaubert's experience as a writer altogether; it caused him to wrestle with nuances of stylistic difference in order to create an idea of complete indifference.

The second achievement of his style is the possibility of a new kind of satirical insight. Perhaps its essence lies in the extraordinary meaning a cliché could have for Flaubert. For a cliché is a phrase from which any real meaning is fast disappearing; it is an idea reduced to the status of a glib fact, a formulation that renders something trite. The novel is full of them, and Bouvard and Pécuchet's entire experience might almost be described as an extended cliché. The satirical significance of a cliché is of the same abstract kind as Flaubert's satire altogether; it is meaninglessness captured purely by the form of expression. Flaubert offsets one experience against another, a theory against its practise and the practise against its outcome, action against motive and motive against statement, Bouvard and Pécuchet's idea of everything and the way they in fact discover it (each after his own fashion, which adds an additional contrast throughout), in order to reveal the inconsequential sameness of it all. It is like an immensely complex and comprehensive mathematical formula which makes everything equal zero. Its significance lies in the way Flaubert formulates every experience in terms that cancel one another out. The terms represent a real enough sequence, but the reckoning is entirely abstract, measuring with exactest precision an essential inconsequence.

One further passage may be quoted in conclusion to illustrate this process. Towards the end of Chapter VIII, Flaubert brings Bouvard and Pécuchet to a point where they apparently attain his own point of view, having developed (into a near-cliché) that 'faculté pitoyable . . . de voir la bêtise et *de ne plus la tolérer*'. They shut themselves up and receive no visitors. But then a wedding invitation arrives and this, of all things, causes them to regret their excess of philosophy and abstract thinking.

The factual report of their solemn thoughts on the subject contrasts with their occasion, with the actual nature of their earlier disillusionment, and with the immediately juxtaposed facts of their simple solution.

> Au milieu de l'été, ils reçurent un billet de faire part annonçant le mariage de Dumouchel avec Mme. veuve Olympe-Zulma Poulet.
> –Que Dieu le bénisse!
> Et ils se rappelèrent le temps où ils étaient heureux.
> Pourquoi ne suivaient-ils plus les moissoneurs? Où étaient les jours qu'ils entraient dans les fermes, cherchant partout des antiquités? . . . Un abîme les en séparait. Quelque chose d'irrévocable était venu.
> Ils voulurent faire, comme autrefois, une promenade dans les champs, allèrent très loin, se perdirent. [1]

The focus shifts for half a sentence to a quite untroubled view of the countryside, and then fixes on the carcass of a dog:

> Les quatre membres étaient desséchés. Le rictus de la gueule découvrait sous des babines bleuâtres des crocs d'ivoire; à la place du ventre, c'était un amas de couleur terreuse, et qui sembler palpiter, tant grouillait dessus la vermine. Elle s'agitait, frappée par le soleil sous le bourdonnement des mouches, dans cette intolérable odeur,–odeur féroce et comme dévorante.
> Cependant Bouvard plissait le front et ses larmes mouillèrent ses yeux.
> Pécuchet dit stoïquement:
> –Nous serons un jour comme ça!
> L'idée de la mort les avait saisis. Ils en causèrent, en revenant.
> Après tout, elle n'existe pas. On s'en va dans la rosée, dans la brise, dans les étoiles. On devient quelque chose de la sève des arbres, de l'éclat des pierres fines, du plumage des oiseaux. On redonne à la Nature ce qu'elle vous a prêté et le Néant qui est devant nous n'a rien de plus affreux que le Néant qui se trouve derrière.

And there, reduced by a series of satirical twists of style to a resounding cliché, is one of the oldest themes of literature. Within two or three pages Bouvard and Pécuchet will,

[1] Ibid., 293 f.

56

literally, have exhausted the subject, prepared philosophically two ropes with which to hang themselves, quarreled then over the slightest domestic incident, attempted suicide, and passed on to a religious conversion. Sometimes a scene is genuinely funny in itself–as when they put off suicide because they have not written their will. But such moments of conventional humour, like others where Flaubert ridicules an idea as absurd in itself, afford only temporary relief from the stylistic satire which renders everything at the same dead level of a spiritually flat reality.

V

Un Cœur simple (1877), the most famous of the *Trois Contes,* is also Flaubert's undisputed masterpiece. Each of the tales concerns sacrifice, in some form that symbolizes the most constant feature of his experience as a writer, the 'martyrdom' of art to the demands of realism; it is present in the sacrifice of St. John the Baptist, in the mortification of St. Julien and, more subtly, in the life of Félicité. The symbolism of her story is made poignant by no dramatic incident, but by the flawless mastery of Flaubert's style. Félicité lacks even the impulse and occasion for romantic action with which Emma deluded herself; her story is of innocence itself, without either the excitement of intrigue or the pathos of disillusionment. She embodies the very simplest qualities of life, life at the bare level of existence. She is, and has always been, a simple servant.

The story opens to show her devotion to a home partly wrapped in dust covers, which shroud the memory of a lost prosperity, its master being dead. She needs only a little garret, some dry bread, and 'erect and silent always, she resembled a wooden figure working automatically': like some enviable article of domestic equipment. Her rude sense of life's realities contrasts with the effete sensitivity of her mistress, Mme. Aubain, her homely, affectionate care of the children with their literary names, Paul and Virginie, and their superior education (which turns the son into a good-for-nothing, and causes the daughter to waste delicately away). So great is her selfless humility that Félicité's life seems too much at one with the world to admit conflict. The description of her deception in love, or her heroic part in helping the family to escape from a bull, is serenely impersonal, as if lacking the focus of conscious experience, suggesting the naiveté of a painting by Douanier Rousseau. On only one occasion in the story does she consciously reflect on her own feelings, in a moment of nostalgic unhappiness, and the moment quickly passes. But gradually Flaubert reveals a real weakness that shall make her the most pathetic victim of his realism. For within her otherwise impersonal existence, she is susceptible to one form of illusion; it is her only spiritual indulgence, her only subjective claim to individuality–and that is her disinterested love, the love of charity.

The irony that will crush her is suggested already in the comment that she loved her weak mistress 'with animal-like devotion and religious veneration'. And it is her selfless, maternal affection for her young nephew, Victor, that leads to her final delusion. When the boy dies in America she obtains from a recently returned sub-prefect, by the only piece of guile of which she was ever guilty, an American parrot as a sentimental souvenir. On this parrot Félicité concentrates all her affection, and it comes to symbolize to her much more than her memory of Victor. Because of a similarity, dimly perceived by her failing eyesight, to the representation in a stained-glass at the church of the Dove of God, the parrot becomes associated in her mind with the Holy Ghost. The bird which was at first 'almost a son, a lover', turns into a religious idol before which she says her prayers.

The end of the story recalls the similar air of desolation in the last chapters of *Madame Bovary*. The home is sold and the sole survivor left, without any purpose in life, to die in a room where the treasured symbols of love contain an unseen irony. She does not suffer any dramatic shock of fatal disillusion like Charles, any more than she can be frightened by some diseased figure of death, like Emma. On the contrary she had tended the cancerous cripple of the village, and dies almost gladly of the same disease that killed her mistress; for the simple fact 'that Madame should die before herself perplexed her mind and seemed contrary to the order of things, absolutely monstrous and inadmissible'. Has Flaubert at last discovered a virtue that can survive the worst that reality can ever be? Or is Félicité too simple-minded in her idea of the 'order of things' ever to be capable of disillusion, as her naive incomprehension of religious doctrine (and perhaps of geography) was surely intended to show? Her fate seems almost worse than that of Emma and Charles, in whose death there was at least a sentimental sense of conventional resolution. By describing meek devotion and humility and self-sacrifice with absolute realism, Flaubert gives to the ambiguity of his style a harrowing power. For the resolution of such suffering and love as Félicité's is made in heaven, and across the very threshold Flaubert draws his most daring line.

In retrospect the whole story appears built to support it. When her parrot dies Félicité overcomes her sorrow, until she can gaze at his stuffed body 'without any sense of bitterness or grief'. When he begins to fall to pieces and her own life is failing, she is already blind and beyond the cares of sense. 'One of his wings was broken, and the wadding was coming out of his body. But Félicité was blind now, and she took him and laid him against her cheek'. Though she can do no more than smell the incense rising from the Corpus Christi service, she participates in the ceremony of divine sacrifice because she has given 'her most treasured possession', the symbol of her love, her parrot, to be laid on the altar. 'And when she exhaled her last breath, she thought she saw in the half-opened heavens a gigantic parrot hovering over her head'.

The Holy Ghost or a pet parrot! The ambiguity is perfectly handled, and sums up the irony of Flaubert's realism. As Félicité concentrated all her affections within this decrepit stuffed bird, so Flaubert had sacrificed all his Romantic inspiration, his intuition of resplendent beauty, his life-long yearning for real poetry, to an impersonal reality—with one wing broken and the stuffing coming out.

APPENDIX

FRENCH

Translation of passages appearing in the text.

p. 42   One day, at the crisis of her illness, when she had really thought that she was dying, she had asked him (Bournisien) to administer Communion. While her room was being prepared for the Sacrament, the chest-of-drawers with its litter of medicine bottles, arranged as an altar, and dahlia blossoms strewn on the floor by Félicité, she felt some powerful influence pass over her which seemed to rid her of all pain, to kill in her all faculty of perception, all ability to feel. Her body, lightened of its burden, had ceased to think. A new life was beginning. She felt as though her being would mount to God and disintegrate in His love, as incense dissipates in vapour.

The sheets of her bed were sprinkled with holy water. The priest took the white Host from the sacred pyx, and, in an almost swooning condition, so great was her joy, she advanced her lips to take the body of her Saviour which he held out for her acceptance. The curtains of the alcove swelled and bellied gently about her like clouds, and the rays of the two candles burning on the chest-of-drawers appeared to her eyes like sunbursts of glory. The ceremony over, she let her head fall back on the pillows, quite convinced that the air was filled with the music of angelic harps, and that she could see mounted on a golden throne within a sky of blue, and surrounded by Saints with green palms in their hands, God the Father shining in majesty, at a sign from whom angels would wing to earth on flaming pinions to take her in their arms upon her final journey.

(*Madame Bovary*, translated from the French by Gerard Hopkins, London, Hamish Hamilton, 1948; p. 258: New York, Dutton, and Oxford University Press, 1949.)

p. 44   'I don't hold it against you', said he [Charles].
Rodolphe remained silent, and Charles, his head in his hands, went on in the same dead voice and the resigned accents of an infinite sorrow.
'No, I don't hold it against you—not any longer'.
He even added the first Great Thought that he had ever voiced:
'It was the fault of Destiny'.
Rodolphe, who, after all, had been the instrument of the said Destiny, felt such an attitude, in a man so placed, was good-natured to excess and, on the whole, rather despicable.   (Ibid., p. 425 f.)

p. 54   The two archaeologists were very shamefaced, and stammered. The object in question was no longer in use.
No matter, they must give it back.
Certainly, but at least they might be allowed to get an artist to come and draw it.
'Very well, gentlemen!'
'This is between ourselves, of course?' said Bouvard. 'Under the seal of the confessional!'

What excitement when the carriage of M. de Faverges stopped before their gate! He had only one word to say. What the matter was, was this:

And from disregard of dates they passed to contempt for facts.

What is important is the philosophy of history.

Bouvard could not finish the famous discourse of Bossuet.
'The eagle of Meaux is a sham. He forgets China, India and America . . .'

(*Bouvard and Pécuchet*, translated by T. W. Earp and G. W. Stonier, Jonathan Cape, London, 1936; pp. 129, 125, 141;) New York, New Directions, 1954.

p. 56   In the middle of the summer they received a formal announcement of Du-mouchel's marriage with Mme Olympe-Zulma Poulet, a widow.
'May God bless him!'
Then they remembered the time when they were happy.
Why did they no longer go out with the harvesters? Where were the days when they went into the farms, looking for antiquities? . . . They were separated from them by an abyss. Something irrevocable had befallen.
They wanted to take a walk in the fields as they used to, went a long way, and got lost.

The four legs were dried up. The grinning jaw revealed ivory fangs beneath blue chops; instead of the belly there was an earth-coloured mass that seemed to quiver, so thickly did it pullulate with vermin. It stirred, beaten by the sun, under the buzzing of flies, in that intolerable stench - a fierce, and as it were, devouring odour.
But Bouvard wrinkled his brow and tears damped his eyes.
Pécuchet said stoically: 'One day we shall be like that'.
The thought of death had taken possession of them. They talked of it as they went back.
After all it does not exist. We depart in the dew, in the breeze, in the stars. We become part of the sap of the trees, the sparkle of jewels, the plumage of the birds. We give back to Nature what she has lent us, and the void before us holds nothing more awful than the void behind us.   (Ibid., p. 259 f.)

BIOGRAPHICAL DATES

1821 12 Dec.   Born in Rouen, second son of a doctor.
1832   Boarder at *collège* of Rouen.
1836 summer   Falls in love with Mme. Elisa Schlésinger at Trouville.
1838   Describes this experience in *Mémoires d'un fou*.
1841 autumn   Enrols in Law Faculty in Paris.
1842 autumn   Finishes *Novembre*.
1843   Friendship with Maxime Du Camp and Schlésingers.
  Begins *L'Education sentimentale* and fails his exams.
1844 Jan.   First attack of recurrent nervous illness.
  June   Family moves to Croisset.
1846   Death of his father and of his sister Caroline.
  Meets Louise Colet.
1847   Travels in Brittany with Du Camp, described in *Par les champs et par les grèves*.
1848 Feb.   Witnesses revolution in Paris.
1849 Sep.   Reads *La Tentation de St. Antoine* to Du Camp and Bouilhet, who condemn it.
  Nov.   Arrives in Alexandria with Du Camp.
1850   Travels in Near East.
1851   At Croisset. Begins *Madame Bovary*.
1856 Oct.   *Madame Bovary* appears serially in *Revue de Paris*.
1857 June   Prosecution of *Madame Bovary*.
  autumn   Begins work on *Salammbô*.
  winter   Visits Carthage.
1858   Retirement to Croisset again.
1862   'Dîners Magny' with de Goncourts, Gautier, Sainte-Beuve (until 1868).
1863   *Salammbô* published. Friendship with George Sand.
1864–69   Work on *L'Education sentimentale*. Lives in Paris during winters. Social fame.
1870   *L'Education sentimentale* published. Grief at deaths of Bouilhet and Sainte-Beuve (1869), Duplan and J. de Goncourt (1870).
1871   Meets Mme. Schlésinger again.
1872   His mother dies. Produces Bouilhet's play and attacks Rouen Municipal Council for refusing a memorial. Finishes third version of *La Tentation* (pub. 1874).
1873   Increasing loneliness in spite of friendship with G. Sand and Turgenev. Plans for *Bouvard et Pécuchet*.
1874   Failure of his play *Le Candidat*.
1875   Mentor to young Guy de Maupassant. Impoverishes himself to save his niece and her husband from financial ruin.
1876   *Trois Contes* (pub. 1877). Death of Louise Colet.
1879   Injured by fall on ice. Friends, including V. Hugo, try to get him a pension; eventually appointed supernumary librarian at the Mazarine.
1880 8 May   Flaubert dies.
1881   *Bouvard et Pécuchet, Oeuvre posthume.*

SHORT BIBLIOGRAPHY

(*cf* also bibliographies by H. P. Thieme (1933), H. Talvert and J. Place
(1928–   ), and S. Dreher and M. Rolli (1948).

I. EDITIONS

Oeuvres complètes de Gustave Flaubert. Conard, Paris, 1910–1936.

II. TRANSLATIONS

Novembre by F. Jellinek (1934).
Madame Bovary by G. Hopkins (1948), by Joan Charles (1949), by Allan Russell (1950).
Salammbô by B. R. Redman (1928), by E. P. Mathers (1931).
L'Education sentimentale by D. K. Ranous (1923), by A. Goldsmith (1941).
La Tentation de St. Antoine (1856 version) by René Francis (1910), and (1874 version)
    by L. Hearn (1911).
Trois Contes by Mervyn Saville (1950).
Bouvard et Pécuchet by T. W. Earp and G. W. Stonier (1936).
Correspondence (with G. Sand) by Aimée L. McKenzie (1922), and a selection by
    J. M. Cohen (1949).

III. WORKS OF REFERENCE

Bertrand, L.: *Gustave Flaubert, avec des fragments inédits.* Paris, 1912.
Canu, J.: *Flaubert, auteur dramatique.* Paris, 1946.
Colling, A.: *Gustave Flaubert.* Paris, 1941.
Demorest, D. L.: *L'Expression figurée et symbolique dans l'œuvre de Gustave Flaubert.*
    Paris, 1931.
Descharmes, R.: *Flaubert avant 1857.* Paris, 1909. *Autour de 'Bouvard et Pécuchet'.* Paris,
    1921.
Dumesnil, R.: *Gustave Flaubert.* Paris, 1932. *Le Grand Amour de Flaubert.* Genèva, 1945.
Faguet, E.: *Flaubert.* Paris, 1906.
Maynial, E.: *Flaubert et son milieu.* Paris, 1927. *Flaubert,* Paris, 1943.
Seillière, E.: *Le Romanticisme des réalistes: Gustave Flaubert.* Paris, 1914.
Spencer, P.: *Flaubert: A Biography.* London, 1952.
Steegmuller, F.: *Flaubert and Madame Bovary,* London, 1947.
Thibaudet, A.: *Gustave Flaubert.* Paris, 1922.

IV. WORKS WITH CHAPTERS ON FLAUBERT

Auerbach, E.: *Mimesis.* Bern, 1946.
Baudelaire, C.: *L'Art romantique* (review of *Madame Bovary,* Ed. Conard).
Boulenger, J.: *Mais l'art est difficile,* II. Paris, 1921.
Bourget, P.: *Essais de psychologie contemporaine.* Paris 1926.
Du Bos, C.: *Approximations.* Paris, 1922.
Gourmont, R. de: *Le Problème du style.* Paris, 1902.
Green, F. C.: *French Novelists, Manners and Ideas.* London, 1928.
James, H.: *Notes on Novelists.* London, 1914.
Proust, M.: *Chroniques.* Paris 1927.
Turnell, M.: *The Novel in France.* London, 1950.
Valéry, P.: *Variété.* Paris, 1944.
Wilson, E.: *The Triple Thinkers.* Oxford U. P. 1938.
Zola, E.: *Les Romanciers naturalistes.* Paris, 1881.

63